ROMULUS

ADAPTED FROM A PLAY OF
FRIEDRICH DUERRENMATT

BY GORE VIDAL

★

═══ A NEW COMEDY ═══

★

DRAMATISTS
PLAY SERVICE
INC.

ROMULUS
Copyright © Renewed 1990, 1989, Gore Vidal
Copyright © Revised 1962, Gore Vidal
Copyright © 1961, Gore Vidal

ALL RIGHTS RESERVED

CAUTION: Professionals and amateurs are hereby warned that performance of ROMULUS is subject to a royalty. It is fully protected under the copyright laws of the United States of America, and of all countries covered by the International Copyright Union (including the Dominion of Canada and the rest of the British Commonwealth), and of all countries covered by the Pan-American Copyright Convention, the Universal Copyright Convention, the Berne Convention, and of all countries with which the United States has reciprocal copyright relations. All rights, including professional/amateur stage rights, motion picture, recitation, lecturing, public reading, radio broadcasting, television, video or sound recording, all other forms of mechanical or electronic reproduction, such as CD-ROM, CD-I, DVD, information storage and retrieval systems and photocopying, and the rights of translation into foreign languages, are strictly reserved. Particular emphasis is placed upon the matter of readings, permission for which must be secured from the Author's agent in writing.

The English language amateur stage performance rights in the United States, its territories, possessions and Canada for ROMULUS are controlled exclusively by DRAMATISTS PLAY SERVICE, INC., 440 Park Avenue South, New York, NY 10016. No non-professional performance of the Play may be given without obtaining in advance the written permission of DRAMATISTS PLAY SERVICE, INC., and paying the requisite fee.

Inquiries concerning all other rights should be addressed to William Morris Agency, Inc., 1325 Avenue of the Americas, 15th Floor, New York, NY 10019. Attn: Owen Laster.

SPECIAL NOTE

Anyone receiving permission to produce ROMULUS is required to give credit to the Author as sole and exclusive Author of the Play on the title page of all programs distributed in connection with performances of the Play and in all instances in which the title of the Play appears for purposes of advertising, publicizing or otherwise exploiting the Play and/or a production thereof. The name of the Author must appear on a separate line, in which no other name appears, immediately beneath the title and in size of type equal to 50% of the size of the largest, most prominent letter used for the title of the Play. No person, firm, or entity may receive credit larger or more prominent than that accorded the Author.

ROMULUS was first presented by Roger L. Stevens in Association with Henry Guettel at The Music Box Theatre in New York City on January 10, 1962. It was directed by Joseph Anthony; the production was designed by Oliver Smith; costumes were by Lucinda Ballard; and the lighting by Peggy Clark. The Associate Producers were Lyn Austin and Victor Samrock. The cast, in order of appearance, was as follows:

TITUS	James Olson
PYRAMUS	Francis Compton
ACHILLES	Russell Collins
ROMULUS	Cyril Ritchard
CHEF	Dolph Sweet
TULLIUS	William Le Massena
APOLLONIUS	Graham Jarvis
JULIA	Cathleen Nesbitt
REA	Suzanne Osborne
METELLUS	George S. Irving
ZENO	Earl Montgomery
AEMILIAN	Ted van Griethuysen
OTTO RUPF	Fred Stewart
OTTAKER	Howard Da Silva
THEODORIC	Edwin Sherin
1ST GOTHIC SOLDIER	Allan Miller
2ND GOTHIC SOLDIER	Dolph Sweet
OTHER GOTHIC SOLDIERS	Drew Elliott, Michael O'Reilly, Harvey Vincent.

PLACE: The villa of the Emperor Romulus at Tivoli, near Rome

TIME: Spring, 476 A.D.

SYNOPSIS OF SCENES

ACT ONE
Morning of March 15th, 476 A.D.

ACT TWO
SCENE 1: One hour later
SCENE 2: Later that night

ACT THREE
Morning, March 16th, 476 A.D.

ROMULUS

ACT ONE

The curtain rises on the audience chamber and garden of the Emperor's villa. The audience chamber should be airy, non-realistic, blending on three sides with a tangled garden of ilex trees and rose bushes gone wild. Upstage a great bronze door opens into the main part of the villa. On the Upstage wall is a pediment supporting a dozen busts of past Emperors; they all look somewhat alarmed. The farthest bust, at stage R. *is of the first Romulus, a choleric-looking man whose eyes are tight shut as though he cannot bear to see what is happening. Above the pediment, directly over the door, is a huge Roman eagle. It seems a perfectly respectable Imperial eagle until one notices that most of its tail-feathers are missing and that the head, instead of glaring off to the* R., *is turned anxiously the other way, looking over its shoulder with a somewhat wild eye, as though fearing an attack from the rear. Beneath the eagle in tall letters upon marble is the legend: SPQR. Downstage* C. *is an outdoor terrace, a step lower than the room. Here a table and two chairs are set. The audience chamber is almost bare with tall arched windows. To stage* R., *a throne is set against the wall. Against the Upstage wall there is a small table on which rests a huge visitors' book, open.*

AS THE CURTAIN RISES, *the stage is empty. Then two ancient courtiers, Pyramus and Achilles, enter from the Upstage door. They start to prepare the room for breakfast (shifting tables, chairs, cushions, rolling on a tea tray with hourglass for eggs, coffee pot, plates, cups, etc.) when they are interrupted by a shout: "Hello!" The courtiers freeze. Then Titus, a young*

Roman officer in uniform, dusty, weary, his tunic stained with blood, staggers into view from stage R. He pauses Downstage, to get his breath. Then he looks about him. He puts his head inside the audience chamber.

TITUS. (*Off.*) Hello . . . ! Hello . . . ! Hey! (*The courtiers do not move.*) Hey! . . . Anybody home? (*Titus crosses to the great room. He steps into it. It takes him a moment to realize that the courtiers are real. He limps wearily to them.*) Thank God! I was afraid nobody was here. (*Deep breath.*) I come from Pavia!
PYRAMUS. (*Drily.*) That is your misfortune.
TITUS. No, I mean I come from the army at Pavia, from General Orestes. I have a message for the Emperor!
ACHILLES. Kindly lower your voice. Romulus Augustus, our Divine Emperor . . . (*Achilles and Pyramus bow their heads and genuflect.*) . . . is still asleep.
TITUS. Well . . . wake him up! I have to see him. Here! (*Pulls forth scroll.*) News from the front. *Urgent* news.
PYRAMUS. Have you an appointment?
TITUS. How could I have an appointment? I come from Pavia!
ACHILLES. He seems obsessed with Pavia.
PYRAMUS. Do you have a name?
TITUS. Titus, Prefect of Cavalry.
ACHILLES. Then sign the visitors' book. (*He indicates book U.*) Your full name . . . (*Titus writes indignantly.*)
PYRAMUS. Military rank . . .
ACHILLES. Place of birth . . .
PYRAMUS. Ambition in life . . . (*Titus flings down the pen in disgust.*)
TITUS. In the name of Heaven, I *must* see the Emperor.
PYRAMUS. (*Reasonably.*) If that is your ambition in life, then write it down.
TITUS. Look here, the news I have is urgent: The Roman Empire is on the verge of total collapse.
PYRAMUS. Don't be melodramatic.
ACHILLES. How can that which is eternal end? (*They continue to prepare for breakfast.*)

PYRAMUS. The Roman Empire is eternal. And therefore: oh, the beauty of classical logic! The Empire cannot end!
TITUS. The Goths are coming! They've broken our defenses!
ACHILLES. For five hundred years the Goths have been on the march to Rome.
PYRAMUS. But they never quite make it to the city.
ACHILLES. Oh, sometimes they get as far as the suburbs.
PYRAMUS. Then they lose interest.
TITUS. Listen, you two . . .
ACHILLES. Careful! We are hereditary Lords of the Bedchamber. . . .
TITUS. Then *please*, Lords of the Bedchamber . . .
PYRAMUS. Most Serene and Illustrious Lords of the Bedchamber is the actual form of address. . . .
TITUS. Oh, God! (*Titus turns away. Pyramus takes pity. He crosses to him.*)
PYRAMUS. Now . . . now, my boy, a career at court cannot be made in a day. You have made a bad first impression—that's true—but don't give up. In two hours, at ten o'clock sharp, the Lord Chamberlain will arrive at his office, that's in the annex—(*Points* R.) across the garden. Write your name in his book, requesting permission for an audience with the Master of the Sacred Household, then present yourself to him, and I predict that you will be received by our Divine Emperor in less than three days' time. (*Titus is defeated. He sighs.*)
TITUS. Unhappy country whose fate depends on two damned dithering idiots! (*Titus runs off through the garden* R. *Pyramus and Achilles look at one another thoughtfully.*)
PYRAMUS. I don't think that young man will be a great success at court.
ACHILLES. I'm afraid he lacks . . .
PYRAMUS. Tone.
ACHILLES. It is curious that as an empire declines there is a noticeable . . . ah, *how* shall I put it?
PYRAMUS. Succinctly.
ACHILLES. A noticeable *decline* in manners. . . .
PYRAMUS. And in values. You are right, dear Achilles. And if I may say so: He who fails to recognize the value the civilization . . . that is to say, the value of you and me, digs the grave of Rome. (*Romulus Augustus enters. He wears a toga*

and on his head the golden wreath of Empire, reduced now to a circlet with only seven gold leaves. Pyramus and Achilles salute and then fall face to the floor, all beautifully executed.)
PYRAMUS and ACHILLES. Hail Caesar!
ROMULUS. Hail!
PYRAMUS. Great is Caesar.
ACHILLES. Magnanimous.
PYRAMUS. Divine.
ACHILLES. All powerful.
PYRAMUS. All wise, Caesar!
ROMULUS. (*Yawns.*) You exaggerate. Is today the Ides of March?
PYRAMUS. Yes, Caesar. Today is the Ides of March.
ROMULUS. Then we must watch our step. (*He comes* D. *The courtiers help him into his toga.*)
ACHILLES. The day according to law . . .
PYRAMUS. And sacred precept . . .
ROMULUS. . . . that all government officials are to be paid. An old superstition. To prevent the Emperor from being murdered. Call the Treasurer. Warn him that it's pay-day.
ACHILLES. The Treasurer has fled, Divine Caesar.
ROMULUS. Fled? Why?
ACHILLES. He hoped by fleeing to conceal the bankruptcy of the Roman Empire.
ROMULUS. That was clever. He who would cover up a great scandal had best create a small one. Pyramus, make a note of what I just said. Posterity will be amused. Where is the Treasurer now? (*Pyramus removes a small notebook, and writes in it. He will often in the course of the play record* mots *of Romulus.*)
PYRAMUS. He has taken a position as salesman with a firm in Syracuse. They sell string.
ACHILLES. He is on what I believe is vulgarly called a "commission basis." . . .
ROMULUS. *Against* a regular salary?
PYRAMUS. Yes.
ROMULUS. Fortunate man!
ACHILLES. (*Horrified.*) But he is in . . . in . . . ah, I cannot say the word!

8

PYRAMUS. I can. He is in *trade*. He can never be received at court again.

ROMULUS. Pyramus, don't be such a snob. After all, I was a professor of history before I married our beloved Empress.

PYRAMUS. You were a great historian, Caesar.

ROMULUS. Until one morning on my way to class I said to myself, why should I teach history when I might become Emperor and make history.

ACHILLES. You are history, Caesar.

ROMULUS. I know. I am the envy of every faculty room in Europe. I am what I used to teach. At times I feel almost mythical. Now to cover immediate expenses, take this. . . . (*He removes wreath and breaks off two leaves.*) One solid 14-carat gold leaf for each of you. Convert them into money, deduct your salaries, and bring me the change.

PYRAMUS and ACHILLES. Such is the will of Caesar!

ROMULUS. (*Looks at wreath.*) Oh, dear! When I took on this job there were thirty-six leaves on this golden wreath, this outward and visible sign of my solvency. Now there are only five. We shall soon be flat broke. (*To Pyramus.*) Breakfast! (*Pyramus rings a bell on the cart and lights burner.* ACHILLES *arranges chair and table downstage. Romulus glances at the visitors' book.*) I see we had a caller this morning, rather early, too.

ACHILLES. A young alarmist. He believes we are in serious danger!

ROMULUS. Does he, indeed? (*To himself.*) So now it begins. (*To them.*) We must not lose our nerve. We are at the razor's edge. Gentlemen, today of all days we wear the mask of comedy.

PYRAMUS and ACHILLES. Comedy?

ROMULUS. (*Nods.*) We must prepare for the unexpected and the bizarre. What is serious we shall make light of. What is frivolous we shall attend with undue solemnity. (*Conspiratorially.*) Gentlemen, be alert. Take your cue from me. (*The Chef enters* L. *with breakfast tray.*) Ah, that looks good. And *three* eggs, too. What a treat! (*He picks up an egg.*) Did my hen Augustus lay this?

PYRAMUS. No, Divine Caesar.

ROMULUS. Tiberius?

PYRAMUS. No, Divine Caesar.
ROMULUS. Not a Claudio-Julian Emperor?
PYRAMUS. No, Divine Caesar.
ROMULUS. Not a Claudio-Julian. Oh, I know, I know! Constantine.
PYRAMUS. Alas, no!
ROMULUS. All right, I give up. Who laid this egg?
PYRAMUS. Marcus Aurelius.
ROMULUS. Such a reliable chicken. Give her an extra ration of corn and confer upon her the title "Savior of the Fatherland." All the other Emperors are worthless, I'm afraid. Did any of them lay? (*During this Romulus puts on gardening gloves and takes up watering can.*)
PYRAMUS. None of our Emperors, no. Only the Gothic Prince . . .
ROMULUS. Ottaker? My competition.
PYRAMUS. (*Nervously.*) I . . . I'm afraid so, Divine Caesar.
ROMULUS. So Ottaker the Butcher laid an egg. (*He waters* D. L. *tub of flowers.*)
PYRAMUS. *Two* eggs, to be absolutely precise. Oh, I know this is terrible news, sir, but . . .
ROMULUS. No, no, no. I am hardened to adversity. And my general of the armies?
PYRAMUS. General Orestes has laid nothing.
ROMULUS. A dud. And my namesake, Romulus?
PYRAMUS. A hen of exquisite proportion, delicious shape, radiant intelligence . . .
ROMULUS. She's a dear hen. But has she laid an egg?
ACHILLES. Almost, Divine Caesar.
ROMULUS. Almost? I believe that is technically impossible. Either a hen lays an egg or she does not. It is rather like that old Greek joke about virginity, either you are or you were, or something like that. I can never remember jokes. Has Romulus laid an egg?
ACHILLES. Not yet, but— (*Romulus marches now from* L. *tub to* R. *tub, which he proceeds to water.*)
ROMULUS. (*Sternly.*) Very well! Those who do not fulfill their function, in this case the laying of eggs, must be sacrificed to the state. I speak now with the voice of many Caesars, all

of us Divine. Tell the chef to cook Orestes, Caracalla, and myself.
ACHILLES. Oh, no!
ROMULUS. Yes! I, too, am fit only for the pot. And in the future I shall eat the eggs of Ottaker the Gothic Butcher.
ACHILLES. But he is the enemy of Rome . . .
PYRAMUS. Of civilization—
ACHILLES. Of good taste—
PYRAMUS. Of classical culture—
ROMULUS. All that is true. He is a fiend. But he lays eggs. We must not allow prejudice to obscure that fact. (*The Lord Chamberlain, Tullius, crosses garden from* R. *He is distraught.*)
TULLIUS. Divine Caesar, Glorious Augustus, Emperor of Rome . . .
ROMULUS. Good morning, Tullius. (*He puts down watering can, removes gloves.*)
TULLIUS. Caesar, a young Prefect, Titus by name, has galloped two days and two nights all the way from Pavia to bring you the news.
ROMULUS. Galloped? All by himself? Without a horse?
TULLIUS. On a horse, Caesar. You knew exactly what I meant.
ROMULUS. Yes, but you expressed yourself imprecisely. (*To Pyramus and Achilles, as he crosses and sits at breakfast table.*) At all times we must speak perfect Latin. Our ablatives, our subjunctives, our genitives are all that we have left to pass on to future generations. Gentlemen, guard your syntax. It is our legacy to generations unborn.
TULLIUS. This young man is near exhaustion, but . . .
ROMULUS. Then put him to bed.
TULLIUS. But, Caesar, his report is earth-shaking.
ROMULUS. My dear Lord Chamberlain, reports never shake the earth. Actions sometimes do. Actions which we cannot control, since they have already happened by the time we get the reports. Reports merely alarm. That is why it is our policy to discourage bad news.
TULLIUS. Caesar!
ROMULUS. (*Serenely.*) Such is the will of the Senate and the people of Rome. SPQR.
TULLIUS. But, Divine Caesar . . .

ROMULUS. You heard me: SPQR. That means I have just made a law. (*Eating egg.*) I'll see the young man in a day or two.
TULLIUS. Caesar, you must . . .
ROMULUS. (*Warningly.*) S-P . . .
TULLIUS. (*As he goes.*) He gets worse and worse.
ROMULUS. Gentlemen, where is the Empress?
ACHILLES. She is in conference, Caesar.
ROMULUS. In conference? So early in the morning? Is she plotting against me?
PYRAMUS. I'm afraid so, Divine Caesar. The Empress is plotting against you.
ROMULUS. Ah, Roman domesticity! (*Apollonius, a Greek art dealer and promoter, enters.*)
APOLLONIUS. Hail! Hail! Hail! Hail, Divine Caesar.
ROMULUS. (*To Pyramus.*) The art dealer at last! Apollonius, you Greek scoundrel. . . .
APOLLONIUS. (*Exuberant.*) Thousand apologies. Three weeks late. But I made it. I got here before the Goths.
ROMULUS. I'd given you up for lost. Where were you?
APOLLONIUS. Alexandria! At an auction. Going, going, gone!
ROMULUS. You prefer an auction to presiding over the bankruptcy of the Roman Empire? Where is your sense of proportion?
APOLLONIUS. I'm just a simple art dealer.
ROMULUS. Simple? I happen to know you had five hundred plaster casts made of that Cicero I sold you.
APOLLONIUS. Well, that was for the Goths. For the high school system they're setting up in the Gothic forests.
ROMULUS. Are the Goths becoming civilized?
APOLLONIUS. Naturally. The whole world wants a classical education. It's the thing. Status. A sign of status. Amo amas amat amamus amatis amant.
ROMULUS. (*Pleased.*) Nice. (*Rising.*) Apollonius, I shall need some money to pay for the decline of the Roman Empire. It's quite costly, declining. You wouldn't think so, but there are so many built-in expenses. At times I can hardly wait for the Fall.
APOLLONIUS. (*Moving after him.*) What have you got? What have you got?

ROMULUS. What have I got? (*Points.*) My predecessors. The busts of all the great Emperors, on sale. A treasure trove!
APOLLONIUS. I'll tell you if they're a treasure trove or not. You don't mind if I take a close look at them. Make sure they aren't fakes. . . . Ha, ha.
ROMULUS. The busts are authentic. However, I cannot guarantee all of the originals. Achilles, fetch a ladder. (*Achilles crosses off* R.)
APOLLONIUS. Actually, the demand for busts isn't what it used to be.
ROMULUS. Oh, here we go again.
APOLLONIUS. My customers prefer Gothic handicrafts. Primitive art is the big thing now. Emperors are a drug on the market.
ROMULUS. (*Pleasantly.*) I wish you had allowed me to say that. (*Achilles has put a small ladder beneath first bust. During the scene Apollonius moves from bust to bust, examining each closely with a magnifying glass. Romulus continues his breakfast. Julia, the Empress, a stern Roman matron, enters from* U. *She approaches Romulus, who continues to eat.*)
JULIA. Hail, Divine Caesar!
ROMULUS. (*Not looking up.*) Hail, Julia, Sovereign Mother of Rome, Empress of every heart, my beloved, darling wife. . . .
JULIA. Don't talk with your mouth full!
ROMULUS. I'm sorry, dear.
JULIA. I have heard a rumor.
ROMULUS. I should have been more surprised if you had *not* heard a rumor. Palaces are designed for rumors. Pyramus, bring our beloved Empress a plate and one of Ottaker's eggs. (*While Pyramus sets her place, the Empress with a sigh sits down.*)
JULIA. I am told that a messenger has arrived from Pavia.
ROMULUS. Have some wine, dear.
JULIA. Well, *what* is the news?
ROMULUS. How should I know? The messenger is asleep.
JULIA. Then . . . wake him up!
ROMULUS. (*He offers her plate.*) Try one of these little rolls. They're delicious.
JULIA. Romulus, you forget that I am . . .
ROMULUS. Darling, not now. Not before breakfast.

JULIA. I am the Empress . . .
ROMULUS. I know, dear. Beloved, adored wife of the *last* Emperor of Rome. . . .
JULIA. (*Fiercely*.) Don't say that. Don't even hint that you are the last.
ROMULUS. Why not? The last Emperor of Rome will occupy a charming place in history. Oh, not admired, of course, and a bit *triste*, but different! I shall be the subject of monographs.
JULIA. You'll be the subject of a Gothic sword if you don't . . . (*Princess Rea, young and pretty, enters from* U.)
REA. Hail, Divine Caesar!
ROMULUS. Oh, good morning. (*Kisses her*.) Hail, darling. (*Rea crosses to her mother*.)
REA. Mother.
JULIA. (*Julia waves her away*.) Rea, your father and I are talking business. . . .
ROMULUS. Nonsense. We're having an egg. Sit down, Rea. (*Rea sits to his* R., *Julia to his* L.)
REA. Did you sleep well, Father?
ROMULUS. I slept marvelously well. It's one of the things I do best. What have you been studying, dear?
REA. I'm memorizing Antigone's lament as she goes to her death. It's awfully tragic.
ROMULUS. Remind me to have your professor banished. Tragedy is proper only in a cold climate. Besides, comedy suits our situation better.
JULIA. (*Beginning*.) Comedy? With Rome in jeopardy? With this poor child's fiancé missing in action. . . .
REA. (*Swiftly*.) Mother, please don't talk about Aemilian.
JULIA. Comedy!
ROMULUS. Yes, comedy. He who is last had best laugh, if I may coin a bit of folk wisdom. (*Achilles enters from* R.)
ACHILLES. Divine Caesar, the Chief of Staff requests audience on a grave matter involving the fate of Rome.
ROMULUS. Audience not granted. I am coining folk wisdom . . . and having breakfast.
JULIA. Achilles, we shall receive the Chief of Staff . . .
ROMULUS. (*Warningly*.) Darling . . .
JULIA. (*Through him*.) . . . in sacred audience (*Achilles bows and goes*.)

ROMULUS. Nero and Caligula murdered their wives with far less provocation.
JULIA. (*Scornfully.*) You are not Nero. Nor Caligula.
REA. Thank Heaven!
ROMULUS. Don't thank Heaven, dear, thank *me*. (*To Julia.*) But I must warn you, I get in a bad temper if breakfast is in any way spoiled by business. (*Metellus, a bone-headed general in armor, enters, salutes.*)
METELLUS. Hail, Divine Caesar!
ROMULUS. Oh, hail, Metellus!
METELLUS. As Chief of Staff, I insist you see the Prefect Titus at once! (*Pyramus meanwhile is whispering in Romulus' ear. Romulus beams. Then he turns to Metellus.*)
ROMULUS. I thought he was asleep.
METELLUS. No soldier can sleep when he knows his country is in danger.
ROMULUS. If that were so we should be a nation of insomniacs and quite useless in battle. (*Julia rises majestically.*) Yes, my darling?
JULIA. You will receive Titus the Prefect. (*Pyramus whispers again in Romulus' ear. He is delighted.*)
ROMULUS. No! Great news! Ottaker . . .
METELLUS. (*Warming up.*) The Gothic monster, the Butcher of Pavia . . .
ROMULUS. No, not that chap. I mean Ottaker my hen has just laid a third egg. It is a record. Pyramus, grant her the title . . .
JULIA. Romulus, the knife is at your throat and you talk of poultry.
ROMULUS. Emperors may come and go, but poultry endures forever. In any case, I don't need to see your wide-awake young Prefect. I am Pontifex Maximus. I read the future. I know auguries. My hen Ottaker has laid three eggs. That means our frontier city of Pavia has fallen to the *real* Ottaker.
PYRAMUS and ACHILLES. Oh!
ROMULUS. Our army is broken.
REA. Father!
JULIA. I don't believe it!
METELLUS. He is right, madame. I didn't want to alarm you at breakfast. But Pavia *has* fallen. The army *is* broken. Gen-

eral Orestes and his entire army have been taken prisoner by the Goths. The Prefect Titus has brought you the last recorded words of General Orestes. Those tragic words are:
ROMULUS. "We shall fight as long as a single drop of blood courses through our veins."
METELLUS. How did you know?
ROMULUS. All my generals say that just before they surrender. Metellus, tell the Prefect to go to sleep. That is an Imperial command, to be disobeyed at his peril. (*Metellus withdraws.*)
JULIA. Romulus, what are we going to do? This is desperate.
ROMULUS. Well, I suppose I shall have to issue a proclamation of some sort, you know, one of those "hold fast for home and hearth" things, that's for the soldiers. . . .
JULIA. Soldiers! If we've lost the army at Pavia, there are no soldiers. They've all gone over to the Goths. Collaborators!
ROMULUS. I shall then make Metellus General of the army.
JULIA. But he's an idiot.
ROMULUS. Only an idiot would want to take over our army at this point. Then, after that command decision, we shall issue a communique about my health. We shall reassure the people that my blood pressure is normal, my arteries unclogged, that I have never been more fit. . . .
JULIA. Yes, a healthy body ruled by an unsound mind.
ROMULUS. Julia! (*He sits bench* L. *Apollonius calls from up between columns number 6 and 7.*)
APOLLONIUS. Three gold pieces for the Ovid.
ROMULUS. Four. Ovid was a great poet.
JULIA. Who is that creature?
ROMULUS. Apollonius of Utica. He's an art dealer. He's buying the statuary.
JULIA. You can't sell them. They are Rome's past.
ROMULUS. Well, Rome's past is up for clearance sale.
JULIA. Those busts, those statues are all that my father the Emperor left behind in this world.
ROMULUS. Not quite all. There is still you, my darling.
APOLLONIUS. All right. Four gold pieces.
JULIA. It's worth five.
ROMULUS. Yes, the Empress is right.
REA. (*She strikes an attitude, partly real, partly play-acting.*)

I'm sorry. I can bear this tragedy no longer. I'm going to study Antigone. I'm going to prepare for the long trip across the Styx to Pluto's dread kingdom. Farewell! (*She exits* U. R.)
ROMULUS. Farewell. Now you've upset the child.
JULIA. Think nothing of it. It's her dramatic lessons. (*Tullius enters from* R., *running.*)
TULLIUS. Hail, Divine Caesar!
ROMULUS. Hail, Tullius. What's the matter now?
TULLIUS. Zeno, the Emperor of Byzantium, begs asylum.
ROMULUS. Zeno? Shouldn't he be home safe in Constantinople?
TULLIUS. No one is safe in this world.
ROMULUS. (*Gently.*) Tullius—please—let *me* make the generalities.
TULLIUS. Sorry, Caesar.
ROMULUS. Where is he now?
TULLIUS. In my office.
ROMULUS. All right, I shall receive him. (*Romulus and Julia go* U. *to thrones.*)
TULLIUS. (*Calling.*) Emperor of Byzantium, we're ready. Caesar's ready! (*Romulus and Julia both arrange their robes like old professionals.*)
ROMULUS. What do you suppose Zeno wants?
JULIA. Our assistance, I suppose. He *is* our cousin.
ROMULUS. *Your* cousin. The Byzantines are your side of the family, not mine. (*Tullius bows; he is about to go off* R., *when Zeno appears, glittering and crowned, like an ikon.*)
ZENO. Greetings! Hail, oh Imperial Brother, fellow Caesar, twin Augustus.
ROMULUS. Oh, hello, Zeno. I must say you're looking very natty. If I'd known you were coming I would've worn *my* Emperor's suit.
ZENO. (*Formally, to Julia.*) Hail to you, Imperial Sister, Empress, Sovereign Mother.
JULIA. We greet you, Imperial Brother, Roman Emperor of the East, Lord of Byzantium— (*Romulus starts to sit; a look from Julia brings him to his feet.*) —Autocrat of Greece.
ROMULUS. (*Sits now.*) Well, Zeno, what can we do for you?
ZENO. First, I must recite the five thousand verses of supplication.

ROMULUS. Oh, God.
ZENO. The ceremony of the Byzantine Court is not only a reflection of the world order, it is order itself.
JULIA. How true!
ROMULUS. How interesting. (*Zeno crosses to them and prostrates himself.*)
ZENO. (*Resonantly.*) Great King, help! Oh, moon of the dark night of this falling universe . . .
ROMULUS. (*To Julia.*) He's very good, isn't he?
ZENO. Help, help, I beseech thee. . . .
ROMULUS. (*Romulus grabs his extended hand.*) Help granted. Congratulations, Zeno, you've done it again. (*Pulls Zeno to his feet.*)
ZENO. I must apologize for my voice.
JULIA. It was never better!
ROMULUS. (*Pulls Zeno into chair.*) Coffee?
ZENO. Please.
ROMULUS. Julia? (*Julia nods; to Pyramus.*) Three. (*To Zeno.*) How nice to see you again.
ZENO. I must say, Romulus, you're a brick to be so nice.
ROMULUS. Nice? Why shouldn't I be? You are Julia's cousin.
ZENO. But we've been at war for seven years.
ROMULUS. At war?
ZENO. But now we must close our ranks against the Goths, the international menace of Gothic-ism.
JULIA. We must, indeed!
ROMULUS. (*Thoughtfully.*) Have we really been at war for seven years? You and I?
ZENO. Of course.
ROMULUS. Why did no one tell me?
JULIA. We did our best, but you would never listen.
ROMULUS. What was our war about *this* time?
ZENO. I took Dalmatia from you.
ROMULUS. Oh? Was Dalmatia mine?
JULIA. Of course it was ours. Dalmatia was my favorite province. Father loved it, too.
ZENO. It is nice, isn't it? Anyway, there Dalmatia was, just sitting there, so I took it. I don't know what got into me. I

couldn't be more sorry. If you like, you can have it back any time.
ROMULUS. Oh, no, my dear fellow. You keep it. I've got quite enough to do right here, around the house. I must confess, Zeno—just between us Emperors—I've been rather out of touch for some time. People don't tell me things any more, and of course I'm awfully busy looking after the chickens . . . so tell me: *Why* did you have to leave Constantinople? Naturally, if you'd rather not talk about it . . .
ZENO. Oh, no, no. Quite all right. My mother-in-law, Verina . . .
JULIA. Charming woman!
ZENO. . . . made a secret alliance with the Goths and together they drove me out.
JULIA. She was always so energetic.
ROMULUS. But I thought you were *pro*-Gothic.
ZENO. Romulus!
JULIA. He has no tact. (*To Zeno.*) The point is that now you are anti-Gothic.
ZENO. That's right. What we must face now is our common danger. Either we hang together or we hang separately.
ROMULUS. (*Startled.*) What?
ZENO. Either we hang together or we hang separately.
ROMULUS. I thought that's what you said. *Very good!* Is it yours?
ZENO. Yes. Thank you. It's from one of my speeches during the 14th Persian War. It's been much quoted.
ROMULUS. I should think so. (*Mutters.*) Hang together . . . hang separately. Very good.
APOLLONIUS. (*Crosses* D.) For the two Gracchi, Pompey, Africanus and Cato, seven gold pieces, eight sesterces.
ROMULUS. Make it an even eight gold pieces.
JULIA. Nine. Not a penny less.
APOLLONIUS. Eight and a half.
ROMULUS. Eight and three-quarters.
JULIA. Nine!
APOLLONIUS. Very well. But in that case I take Marius and Sulla, too. (*Apollonius exits* L.)
JULIA. Romulus, that junk-dealer is a cheat.
ROMULUS. Junk? You call our classical heritage junk?

Really! Anyway, we need Apollonius more than he needs us. We must have money to pay our debts. I insist on settling every account before the end.
JULIA. The end?
ROMULUS. The end of the month.
ZENO. Apparently I am the only one here who is fully aware of the international menace of Gothic-ism.
JULIA. No, I am, Zeno. Every day I plead with him to take things seriously, to make plans. Zeno, you must help me convince him that the end of the world is not a laughing matter, but bitter.
ZENO. I'll do my best. Romulus, the Goths are winning.
ROMULUS. Yes, even I am aware of that.
ZENO. Now! *Why* are they winning?
JULIA. Because we have no one to lead us. Because we have an Emperor who is indolent, and facetious.
ROMULUS. (*Gently.*) Darling, do let Zeno answer his own question. People always prefer to answer their own questions, otherwise they wouldn't ask them.
ZENO. Thank you. Now the main reason we're losing is because we don't have a proper . . . slogan.
ROMULUS. Slogan?
ZENO. Yes. The Goths are doing quite well with "Progress and Slavery." So I would suggest . . . oh, I know you may think me old-fashioned, but I would suggest: "For Slavery and God."
ROMULUS. Yes, it's catchy. But I'm not so sure God is on our side these days. (*Looks up.*) I rather think there is an agonizing reappraisal going on.
JULIA. What about "Right versus Wrong?"
ROMULUS. A bit too simple. They could use it, too. I prefer something more practical in the way of a slogan, something . . . constructive. Like "For Better Agriculture, Better Poultry!"
JULIA. Don't be smart-aleck!
ZENO. We're also losing because we no longer believe in the Roman way of life. Unless we pull ourselves together and believe absolutely and totally in our manifest destiny, we shall fail.
JULIA. Hear, hear!

ROMULUS. All right, then. Let us believe.
ZENO. What?
ROMULUS. You suggest that we must believe in the Roman way. Very well, I'm willing to give it a try. So: *let us believe.* Ready? Set? Now: all together: Believe! (*A moment of silence.*)
ZENO. You're believing, aren't you?
ROMULUS. Yes, I am believing.
ZENO. Especially in our ancient greatness?
ROMULUS. Particularly in that.
ZENO. And you . . . you believe in our manifest destiny to rule the world?
ROMULUS. (*Ticks them off.*) Manifest destiny . . . rule the world . . . right.
ZENO. And you, Empress?
JULIA. I have always believed in the Roman Way.
ZENO. It's a marvelous feeling, isn't it? All this belief. You can't help feeling that something's happening, right now, in this room, with us really believing in ourselves. At last!
JULIA. At last. Belief.
ROMULUS. And now what?
ZENO. (*Opens eyes.*) What do you mean, and now what?
ROMULUS. Well, since we all believe . . .
ZENO. Then that's it. That's all there is.
ROMULUS. But what exactly are we to *do?*
ZENO. The petty details can be left to others.
ROMULUS. But don't you think that now we are in this . . . extraordinary frame of mind, we ought to do something? You know, like save the Roman Empire?
JULIA. (*She rises.*) Zeno, it's worked. He believes!
ZENO. Salvation will now happen quite naturally of its own accord. (*Metellus rushes in from* R.)
METELLUS. (*Off.*) Caesar! (*Coming on.*) Caesar, the Goths are marching on the city of Rome!
ZENO. (*Just up* R. *of Romulus.*) Marching on Rome?
JULIA. (*Just up* L. *of Romulus.*) Marching on Rome?
METELLUS. I have ordered every man to hold fast.
JULIA. (*Crossing to Metellus.*) Any man who runs away will be executed. That's an order. (*Julia and Metellus look off* U. R.)
ZENO. (*To Romulus.*) When's the next ship for Alexandria?

ROMULUS. Eight-thirty, I think. There's a time-table on my desk. But won't it be awfully hot in Africa this time of year? Especially in those clothes.
JULIA. (*Desperately.*) Romulus, the Goths are at our gates. Do something. Anything!
ROMULUS. Very well, I shall do "anything." Metellus! (*Metellus steps to him.*) I promote you to General of all the armies of Rome. In the field, in the barracks, and in flight.
METELLUS. I shall save Rome, Divine Caesar.
ROMULUS. Exactly what I had in mind. You are perceptive.
METELLUS. But I must insist on one thing: Total mobilization.
ROMULUS. Total mobiliz—what sort of phrase is that?
METELLUS. I just invented it. It means the entire country must concentrate on nothing but the war effort.
ROMULUS. Oh, no. No. I don't like that, even as a matter of style.
ZENO. (*Steps in.*) But the General's right. Only this total . . . thing can save our culture from Gothic-ism.
ROMULUS. The idea is completely absurd. Nevertheless, I bow to necessity. For you, General, I shall mobilize totally. And I put at your disposal the palace guard consisting of nine men and twelve officers. They are yours.
METELLUS. But Ottaker has an army of a hundred thousand well-trained Gothic troops.
ROMULUS. The greater the General, the fewer the troops he needs.
METELLUS. Never was a general of Rome so humiliated by his Emperor! (*Metellus marches Off* R.)
JULIA. I shall mobilize the defense of the palace! (*She starts Off* U. *Apollonius enters* L.)
APOLLONIUS. I'll give you twenty gold pieces for everything. Not a cent . . .
JULIA. Twenty-five! (*Julia goes.*)
APOLLONIUS. All right, twenty-five. For you, I'll make it twenty-five. But that's for the whole mess.
ROMULUS. It's a deal. But I want cash. Now.
APOLLONIUS. Okay, okay. But I'm leaving one bust. That one there in the entry, the first Romulus.
ROMULUS. The founder of Rome? Why?

APOLLONIUS. Bad workmanship. If you'll notice, he's starting to crumble.
ROMULUS. How you Greeks love a symbol!
ZENO. Who is this fellow?
ROMULUS. Apollonius of Utica, I present the Emperor of Byzantium.
APOLLONIUS. How do you do, sir.
ZENO. (*Impressed.*) Not *the* Apollonius of "Apollonius Fine Arts Limited"?
APOLLONIUS. That is I.
ZENO. Well . . . well . . . this is an honor, I must say. I get your catalogs regularly. You buy estates, don't you?
APOLLONIUS. And sell them.
ZENO. Oh, I know, I know. You must pay a visit to the Island of Patmos, a dear little place which still belongs to me, I think. I have a great many original Greek statues there, in the palace. . . .
APOLLONIUS. Happy to appraise them for you. At a nominal, nominal charge, of course.
ZENO. I wondered if perhaps you might not be able to make me a small advance, just as a token of . . .
APOLLONIUS. Sorry! No advances to royalty. Rule of the house. And now, Divine, Divine Caesar, I gotta get going. Don't want the Goths to catch me.
ROMULUS. Certainly . . . certainly. I couldn't apologize more, having you here just as everything breaks up. Just one more thing. (*Takes Apollonius* D. C., *indicates eagle above.*) How much for the Imperial Eagle? (*Julia enters* U. C. *with Pyramus and Achilles.*)
APOLLONIUS. Nothing. It's lost too many feathers. (*Pyramus and Achilles move down to remove throne off* L. *Julia moves down to* L. *of* C.)
ROMULUS. So it has. How odd! I hadn't noticed before. It's also looking the wrong way. In fact, that bird seems quite alarmed.
JULIA. Everyone—even the bird—is alarmed.
ROMULUS. (*Crosses to her.*) Julia, what are you doing with my throne?
JULIA. It's being shipped to Sicily. It was father's
ROMULUS. Why Sicily?

JULIA. Because that is where I intend to set up your government-in-exile.
ROMULUS. Nero and Caligula were right.
APOLLONIUS. Well, I'm off. I'll send my packers round for the busts. (*To Zeno.*) Nice to meet you, Emperor. (*To Romulus.*) Emperor. (*To Julia.*) Madame. See you in Sicily. See you in exile. Got to flee now. Going, going, gone! (*He exits U. R.*)
ZENO. Absolutely nobody, nobody will give me credit. Romulus, we are in an impossible profession.
TULLIUS. (*Off.*) Oh! oh . . . !
ROMULUS. It gets more impossible every moment. (*Tullius enters from U. C.*)
TULLIUS. (*Moving down to Romulus.*) Divine Caesar, hail!
ROMULUS. Hail, Tullius.
TULLIUS. He's here! Otto Rupf is here. Right here, in your palace!
ROMULUS. Why?
TULLIUS. He wrote you a letter, Divine Caesar, asking for an audience.
ROMULUS. You know I don't read letters.
ZENO. Who is Otto Rupf?
JULIA. A true patriot.
TULLIUS. A good Roman. And a great human being.
ROMULUS. But, unfortunately, he makes pants.
ZENO. He makes *what?*
ROMULUS. A new garment worn about the legs. Sometimes called trousers. It's the latest thing, if you're a Goth.
TULLIUS. Romans wear them, too.
ROMULUS. But not in my presence. It is one of the few things I am firm about. I have never seen this hideous garment, and I pray that I never shall. I regard its inventor, Otto Rupf, as un-Roman. We shall not see him, Tullius.
JULIA. You must.
ROMULUS. Why?
JULIA. Because he is the richest man in the world.
ROMULUS. I fail to see what the one has to do with the other.
JULIA. You will. (*To Tullius.*) Show him in. (*To Romulus.*) Money can do anything.
ROMULUS. Can it? I must give the matter some thought. You

have become quite a philosopher, Julia, in our declining years. Very well, I shall see this Otto Rupf.
TULLIUS. (*Calling.*) Mr. Rupf! We're ready. Mr. Otto Rupf! (*Zeno and Romulus set up the throne. Romulus is barely seated when Otto Rupf enters* U. *He is a plump, ovoid businessman, wearing rimless spectacles and a peculiar-looking blouse which resembles nothing so much as the coat of a double-breasted suit. At his throat is a garish bit of cloth, suspiciously like a necktie. His trousers, however, have been removed and his shirttail falls forlornly to the knees, while his spindly legs are ornamented with garters of the most modern kind. Over his shoulders he wears a polo coat of the sort affected by heads of motion picture studios. The effect at first should be in the general style of the play; then as we take in details the anachronism becomes more obvious. He carries a Homburg.*)
ROMULUS. (*Inadvertently.*) Good God! I mean, welcome, Otto Rupf.
RUPF. (*Firmly.*) Emperor.
JULIA. Dear Mr. Rupf, what a nice surprise.
ROMULUS. In the name of the Senate and People of Rome we extend you greetings. SPQR—*What* on earth are you wearing?
RUPF. More to the point, what am I *not* wearing. I was told it was a rule of your court that no one approach you wearing trousers. So I took my pants off in the lobby.
JULIA. Oh, I *am* sorry.
RUPF. (*Ignores Romulus. To Julia.*) Well, Empress. I got your letter. And I'm here.
JULIA. Oh, you are good.
ROMULUS. Letter?
JULIA. Generous.
ROMULUS. What letter?
JULIA. Kind.
RUPF. (*Ignoring him again.*) *Now* I guess you know me, Emperor. Our firm, my family's firm, has been in textiles for over two hundred years. I guess you might say I'm the biggest textile manufacturer in the world.
ROMULUS. I might very well say that. In fact I *will* say it: You are the biggest . . . textile manufacturer in the world.
RUPF. As a pants manufacturer—that's our big specialty—I

am here to tell you that if Rome won't wear pants, Rome will fall. The Goths wear pants. They're conquering the world. Therefore, pants are the wave of the future.
ROMULUS. You may be right. But now I assume you did not come here to sell me a pair of trousers.
RUPF. Now then: We have here on the one hand the richest man in the world . . .
JULIA. You!
RUPF. Me. On the other hand, we have the Roman Empire, a complete bust. That's you.
ROMULUS. You have a gift for precise analysis.
RUPF. Now, for a while there I was thinking maybe I'd buy your Empire.
ROMULUS. (*Excited, pleased.*) You were? Really? Oh, my dear fellow, we must have a serious talk. Yes, indeed, a really serious talk. You were right, Julia, about money.
RUPF. (*Through him.*) No, no. You got me wrong. I'm not going to buy.
ROMULUS. Oh, dear! And for a moment I'd hoped . . .
RUPF. No. I decided your Empire's not a good property. It would cost a fortune just to renovate it and even then who knows if we'd ever make a cent of profit. No, I'm against buying, even at sacrifice prices. But I'm not against . . . merger.
ROMULUS. But how do you propose we merge your excellent business with my somewhat seedy Empire?
RUPF. Your trouble is you don't think big. You don't think organically. To be a success you've got to think organically, step by step. Now, first step: Get the Goths out of Italy, that's A-Number-One on the agenda.
ROMULUS. But won't that be a bit difficult? I mean, suppose they don't want to go?
JULIA. Mr. Rupf can do anything.
RUPF. Nothing is difficult if you got ready cash.
JULIA. Oh, you're so right. (*To Romulus.*) He's so right.
RUPF. I been in touch with Ottaker. I made him a tentative offer. For ten million he'll go back where he came from. And I got it in writing.
ROMULUS. (*Startled.*) Ottaker?
RUPF. That's right. For ten million, he goes home.
JULIA. You see?

ROMULUS. Odd? I should have thought that he, of all people, would be incorruptible. The whole point to monsters is that they are sincere.

RUPF. Sincere or not, you can buy anybody, Emperor. Just a matter of price.

ROMULUS. You have shattered my last illusion. What do you want from me in exchange for your assistance?

RUPF. I'm willing to pay off Ottaker. I'll even toss a few million into the kitty. You know, just to get the old show going again. But, in exchange, everybody, but everybody's *got* to wear pants.

JULIA. The least we could do.

ROMULUS. I would have said it was the most. (*To Rupf.*) And what else?

RUPF. I marry your daughter, Rea. Thereby cementing our merger organically.

ROMULUS. (*Coldly.*) I'm sorry.

JULIA. Romulus!

ROMULUS. My daughter is engaged to be married to a young patrician . . .

JULIA. Who has been a Gothic captive for nine years. . . .

ROMULUS. Captive or not, she loves him. . . .

JULIA. How could she love him? She was a child when they were betrothed.

ROMULUS. (*To Julia.*) I'm sorry. (*To Rupf.*) I'm afraid, Mr. Rupf, we must decline your offer and continue with our . . . fall.

RUPF. (*On his own track.*) I hope you got the picture: If you don't merge with a solid firm like mine, your empire's had it and Gothic-ism has won the struggle for men's minds, like they say.

TULLIUS. Yes, yes.

ROMULUS. Good day, Mr. Rupf.

RUPF. (*To Julia.*) Well, Empress, looks like you got me here under false pretenses.

JULIA. No, no!

RUPF. (*To Romulus.*) I ought to warn you if I get a turn-down from you I'll marry Ottaker's daughter.

JULIA. (*Intensely.*) Mr. Rupf, you wouldn't—you *couldn't* do that. You mustn't listen to my husband. He's not himself these days.

RUPF. The Rupf firm has got to have an heir. And a Gothic connection makes a whole lot more sense than a Roman one, organically speaking. But I got this sentimental streak.

JULIA. You love our daughter. What could be more natural?

RUPF. (*Thoughtfully.*) The daughter of the Caesars *would* give a lot of tone to company parties. The big wholesalers are suckers for royalty. Especially the Chinese. That's right, I'm out to land the Chinese account. I think big!

JULIA. You *are* big! That is why you inspire us all.

ROMULUS. Good day, Mr. Rupf.

JULIA. (*Softly.*) Don't go. Tullius, look after dear Mr. Rupf, and show him everything, while we discuss this happy event.

TULLIUS. I shall be happy to show you everything, anything.

RUPF. Now while you're making up your mind, I'd like to see the books. I want a complete inventory of the empire: assets, deficits, mortgages, tax structure, the overall *organic* picture.

ZENO. Mr. Rupf, I am the Emperor of Byzantium. Have you ever been to the Island of Patmos? (*Rupf and Tullius go off R., pursued by Zeno. Romulus starts to go U.*)

JULIA. Romulus, come here. You cannot escape this.

ROMULUS. Escape?

JULIA. Whether you like it or not, Rea must marry Mr. Rupf. Now. Before he changes his mind. Before the Goths arrive.

ROMULUS. I was quite prepared for a nominal sum to sell the Empire to your friend . . . and pen-pal. But I will not give him my daughter for all . . . for all the tea in China.

JULIA. *You* might not, but think of Rea. She is a patriotic Roman girl. She would sacrifice herself gladly to save us.

ROMULUS. But I won't let her.

JULIA. Rea is a small price to pay for Rome.

ROMULUS. As usual, you are so maternal.

JULIA. It is the end of the world if Rea does *not* marry Otto Rupf.

ROMULUS. You mean it is *our* end. Which is not precisely the same thing.

JULIA. We are the world!

ROMULUS. Hardly. We are poor country cousins in a strange

new era, where people speak a different language and wear pants.

JULIA. I don't understand you.

ROMULUS. I know you don't.

JULIA. I have never understood you.

ROMULUS. Many happy marriages have been based upon complete mutual misunderstanding.

JULIA. Happy!

ROMULUS. I am given to hyperbole.

JULIA. (*Gestures at room.*) Look at what has become of us! When I was a girl, this shabby room glittered with attendants, courtiers, statesmen. This was the center of the earth, right here, and I was proud, oh, so proud, to be the daughter of Caesar.

ROMULUS. Then after many years of exquisite pride, you married me.

JULIA. Yes. And ever since I have had to watch day by day the world that was ours shrink to this one house . . . to dust, cobwebs, empty rooms . . .

ROMULUS. Come now, it may be a bit run-down, but it's still home.

JULIA. (*Exploding.*) *Why do you always mock us?*

ROMULUS. (*Evenly.*) I mock what is false. I honor what is true.

JULIA. Well, *this* is true: Otto Rupf can save us. It is also true that if you try to stop him, others will stop you!

ROMULUS. Is that a threat?

JULIA. That is a threat.

ROMULUS. Be careful, Julia. Be very careful. The comedy is a mask. The face is one you have never seen. If you stand in my way, even *I* may turn monster.

JULIA. Is that a threat?

ROMULUS. That is a threat. You must not interfere.

JULIA. Then, in the name of Heaven, *what* do you plan to do?

ROMULUS. Nothing.

JULIA. I am ashamed to be your wife! (*Julia goes. Romulus calls after.*)

ROMULUS. But I do have a plan. (*Julia laughs mockingly as she exits. To himself.*) I have always had a plan. From the very beginning. And I must not fail. (*Pyramus and Achilles enter* L.,

Achilles with bowl and towel.) Oh? Yes, Pyramus, I am finished. (*He washes his hands in bowl, as Titus enters from* U. R.)
TITUS. Hail, Caesar!
ROMULUS. Hail. Who are you? (*Romulus dries his hands.*)
ACHILLES. This is not polite, young man.
PYRAMUS. This is not done. (*Titus drops on his knees in front of Romulus.*)
TITUS. I'm Titus. Prefect from the army.
ROMULUS. How do you do?
TITUS. For two days and two nights I've ridden. Seven horses died beneath me. I am wounded, and yet when I got here *they* wouldn't let me see you.
ACHILLES. He had no appointment. (*Titus draws a scroll from his belt.*)
TITUS. Divine Caesar, here is the last message of your last General as he was taken prisoner by the Goths.
ROMULUS. (*Taking the scroll.*) How extraordinary! Just look at you: exhausted, wounded . . . Why do you put yourself to all this trouble, when you should be in bed?
TITUS. That Rome may live!
ROMULUS. (*Romulus rises.*) No one has yet found a way to raise the dead.
TITUS. But Rome's not dead. There's still us!
ROMULUS. You? Me? Against all of history? (*Romulus starts to go* R. *Titus rises.*)
TITUS. But what about my country . . . ? (*Romulus turns, between contempt and pity.*)
ROMULUS. You have no country. Don't you see? Time has played a trick on you. You were born too late to change the awful past and born too soon to make a better future. We are in no-man's land. Get some rest, Prefect.
TITUS. Caesar, we must fight!
ROMULUS. Fight? For what? (*Romulus drops the scroll, then exits.*)
TITUS. (*To Pyramus and Achilles.*) But that can't be the Emperor. . . . (*Pyramus and Achilles exit* L.) This is a dream. . . .

CURTAIN

ACT TWO

Scene 1

Smoke from R. *Tullius is working. Metellus is on the bench asleep. Titus runs in from* U. R.

TITUS. Smoke! Smoke! Hey, what's happening? What's on fire?
TULLIUS. We're burning the archives.
TITUS. But . . . (*Stops, looks at foot.*) Oh, I stepped on an egg. What a mess! This damned cackling and nobody doing anything. Anything!
TULLIUS. Speak for yourself. *I* am making plans for the government's removal to Sicily. You have no idea what a lot of paper work that involves. And General Metellus there is working on his plan of battle.
TITUS. Plan of battle? He's sound asleep! Everybody's asleep.
TULLIUS. I certainly wish you were. (*Titus gestures toward* U. *door.*)
TITUS. There couldn't be an Emperor like that. Could there?
TULLIUS. There could be and there is. He's quite unorthodox in his ways. I suppose that's because he's an intellectual. They say his books are brilliant, especially "The Moral Principle in History." But I couldn't get through it. Of course, he's from one of the best families. That's why the Empress had to marry him because though her father was Emperor, her mother was a slave, and only by marrying a patrician could *she* become Empress. Oh, I love genealogy!
TITUS. He said I had no country. He's crazy.
TULLIUS. Yes. That's quite possible. In fact, if it weren't for the Empress, there wouldn't be an Empire now. She keeps the whole thing going.
TITUS. I'm right. This is a dream. Look, I can walk through

this pillar, through solid stone. See? It isn't real. Nothing's real. (*His head bangs into the pillar.*) Ow!
TULLIUS. It's real. Our great hope was Aemilian, a young patrician at court. He was engaged to marry the Princess. We all hoped he would take over one day, but he's been missing in action for years and . . . (*The Chef enters from* U. R. *with three dead chickens and a knife.*)
CHEF. By Imperial decree the menu for today, the 15th of March, 476 A.D. Filet de sole Normande. Poularde aux truffes Romulus. Salad Verte. Bombe glace Julia. Will you look at these scrawny chickens? Supposed to be broilers. They are an insult to my talent. An affront to my art. I, who once made thirty-course dinners for sittings of five hundred, am now reduced to these. Oh, the world is ending! My kitchen is cold. My pots, my pans reproach me. I cannot face my stove. (*He exits* L.)
TULLIUS. He's very good with leftovers. (*Metellus stirs on his bench.*)
METELLUS. Shut up!
TULLIUS. Yes! You mustn't talk so loud. General Metellus needs his sleep if he's to save us from the Goths. (*Titus sits, wretchedly.*)
TITUS. The cackling . . . my nerves . . .
TULLIUS. Do stop complaining. And stop fidgeting. (*Metellus sits up, angrily.*)
METELLUS. Look, I am trying to think. To concentrate. To make a plan of battle, while you keep chattering like a . . . (*He picks up a shield with "Progress and Slavery" scribbled on it.*) Who wrote that on my shield?
TULLIUS. Oh, they've written it all over everything.
METELLUS. Here in my own headquarters, Gothic agents write Gothic slogans on my own shield! Tullius, we are surrounded by spies and traitors! (*He springs to his feet.*)
TULLIUS. I'm afraid so, General.
METELLUS. I want a complete investigation by the Senate. It's incredible! Un-Roman activities right here in the palace. I've had enough of this coddling of Goths. We must root out all subversives! (*To Titus.*) Prefect, mobilize totally!
TITUS. Yes, sir. But how, sir?
METELLUS. That's an order!

TULLIUS. But, General, the big problem at the moment is: How do we get to Sicily?
METELLUS. To Sicily? We shall fight as long as a single drop of blood courses through our veins.
TULLIUS. (*Reasonably*.) Of course we will. But *first* we must escape. For the sake of civilization. You see, I've just completed plans for reorganizing the Empire. We have a great deal of social legislation we plan to enact. We also plan to eliminate the graduated income tax *while* increasing military expenditures at the same time. Now, how's that for a program?
METELLUS. Civilians!
TULLIUS. But none of these marvelous things can be done if we don't get a boat.
METELLUS. Well, order a three-master.
TULLIUS. We can't afford one. But we can just about swing a second hand galley, *if* we get a good enough break price-wise. I wish you'd see to that, General. There's one for sale over in Trastevere.
METELLUS. Now I'm a travel agent.
TULLIUS. I'm sorry, General.
METELLUS. I, who might have been a greater general than Julius Caesar, than Alexander the Great . . . (*Metellus is about to leave* L. *when the Empress appears* U. C.)
JULIA. You *are* as great a general as Alexander, Metellus. It's not your fault that the Emperor has given you no support.
METELLUS. Nevertheless, madame, I shall do my duty. No matter how harsh. (*Julia comes* D.)
JULIA. Both you and Tullius will do your duty, won't you?
TULLIUS. Naturally, Divine Empress. (*Titus joins them, and drops to his knees before Julia.*)
TITUS. And so will I! But what *is* our duty, Empress?
JULIA. Our duty is to persuade the Emperor that he must allow the Princess to marry Otto Rupf.
TULLIUS. But the Emperor said "No." He seemed unusually firm about that. . . .
JULIA. But we might change his mind, mightn't we?
METELLUS. He's very stubborn, madame.
JULIA. (*Pointedly*.) We can be stubborn, too. (*To Metellus.*) No matter what happens today, will you stand with me . . . for Rome?

METELLUS. (*Kneels.*) Yes, madame.

JULIA. (*To Tullius.*) And you?

TULLIUS. (*Kneels.*) I, yes, Divine Empress.

TITUS. And so will I, Empress. I'll kill any traitor you ask me to. Including the Emperor.

JULIA. (*Simulating a girlish flutter.*) Oh, dear. I didn't hear that. I did *not* hear that. But I admire your spirit, Prefect. You are what we are fighting for: Youth! Be on your guard, gentlemen. We shall save Rome yet. (*Julia exits* R.)

METELLUS. (*Admiringly.*) She *is* Rome. Prefect, whatever she asks us to do, we shall do. But just to be on the safe side, I'll check on that galley. (*Metellus exits* L.)

TULLIUS. (*Glumly.*) Well, it looks like a coup d'etat to me. How I hate them! Whenever you murder an Emperor, the files get so mixed up, and you have to rewrite the history books again. Oh, it's going to be total confusion.

TITUS. (*Stretches wearily.*) Well, I'll do anything. Anything she asks me to do. . . . If only I can keep awake. (*Titus settles down next to a pillar. Chickens cackle loudly. Aemilian, a tattered, worn, exhausted young man, enters. He looks about.*)

AEMILIAN. (*Softly.*) The palace of the Roman Emperor.

TULLIUS. (*Starts.*) Who are you? You're not a Goth, are you?

AEMILIAN. I'm a ghost.

TULLIUS. What do you want?

AEMILIAN. My father.

TULLIUS. His name?

AEMILIAN. The Emperor. He's the father of us all, isn't he?

TULLIUS. Of every patriot. In fact, the word "patriot" derives from "pater," which means . . .

AEMILIAN. So I am a patriot. And I have come to my father's house. (*Looks about.*) A filthy farm house. Chickens underfoot. Eggs in every bush, and somewhere an Emperor, taking his afternoon nap.

TULLIUS. You seem acquainted with court life. However, you must first sign the book. Then I suggest you request audience . . .

AEMILIAN. Hello, Tullius.

TULLIUS. How do you know my name?

AEMILIAN. We've been at many parties together, you and I.

TULLIUS. I rather doubt that.
AEMILIAN. Of course it was a long time ago. One world ago, to be exact!
TULLIUS. Where are you from?
AEMILIAN. Reality. I have come from the modern world to this . . . charade.
TULLIUS. That means you're a veteran. I recognize the tone. So bitter. What can we do for you?
AEMILIAN. Defeat the Goths, that's what you can do.
TULLIUS. Well, we're working on that right now. Naturally, it's quite a long-range project, battle of men's minds, you know, basically a war of ideas. . . .
AEMILIAN. I see you can do nothing for me.
TULLIUS. Oh, I grant you there is an element of tragedy in what is happening. And I do feel at times that perhaps a chapter is ending but not, if I may complete the metaphor, the book itself. We shall win as we have always won. Our higher culture will defeat Gothic-ism.
AEMILIAN. (*Suddenly.*) You like Horace. You write the best prose, both Greek and Latin.
TULLIUS. Naturally. I am a lawyer.
AEMILIAN. I liked Horace. I wrote perfect Latin, perfect Greek.
TULLIUS. Are you a poet?
AEMILIAN. When there was poetry, I was poet.
TULLIUS. Then write poems again. "Of arms and the man, I sing." (*Starts to write.*)
AEMILIAN. But where I have been there was no poetry. There was death. I was dead. (*Rea enters from* R., *declaiming.*)
REA.
> "Thebes, and you my father's gods,
> And rulers of Thebes, you see me now, the last
> Unhappy daughter of a line of kings,
> *Your* kings, led away to death."

TITUS. Nothing puts me to sleep faster than the classics. (*Titus reels Offstage* R. *Rea turns, still play-acting, to Aemilian.*)
> "you will remember what things I suffer, and at what men's hands

Because I would not transgress the laws of Heaven.
Come: Let us wait no longer."
(She motions to Aemilian as though he were a fellow character.)
AEMILIAN. *(Pause.)* Who are you?
REA. Antigone, going to her death.
AEMILIAN. No, I mean who are *you?*
REA. I should ask you that. You are the stranger.
AEMILIAN. I'm a ghost.
REA. *(Matter-of-fact.)* Oh? I'm not at all surprised. The last few days the omens have been dreadful. At Ostia a calf was born two-headed. Toads fell in the rain this morning. And now they say the spirit of Rome was seen last night in the Forum, weeping and covered with ashes. Yes, I am certain you are a ghost. But then, we shall all be ghosts soon enough. I am Rea, "unhappy daughter of a line of kings."
AEMILIAN. *(Softly.)* Rea. I didn't recognize you. You are beautiful. But I forgot your face.
REA. Have we met before?
AEMILIAN. Yes, when I was alive.
REA. Did you live in Ravenna? Did we play together when we were children?
AEMILIAN. We played together. In Ravenna. We were children.
REA. What is your name?
AEMILIAN. You will see it written in my left hand. *(He holds out his hand.)*
REA. It's horrible . . . all scarred . . .
AEMILIAN. Shall I take it back?
REA. I can't look.
AEMILIAN. Then you will never know who I am.
REA. Give me your hand. . . . Your . . . poor, wounded, crippled hand. *(She extends her right hand; he puts his left on hers.)* But . . . *that's* Aemilian's ring.
AEMILIAN. *(Nods.)* The ring of the man you were to marry.
REA. The skin has grown round the ring. . . .
AEMILIAN. Yes. It has become one with the burnt flesh.
REA. You are Aemilian.
AEMILIAN. I was.
REA. Are you really a ghost?

AEMILIAN. Touch me. (*Rea puts her hand on his bare arm. She caresses him, at first tentatively.*)
REA. You are warm.
AEMILIAN. So is the fire in hell. (*Rea touches his face, his lips. Unable to control himself, he seizes her hand and presses it hard to his mouth.*)
REA. (*Ecstatic.*) Aemilian! (*Rea throws herself into his arms. He holds her tight.*)
AEMILIAN. But I'm not Aemilian. I'm not what I was.
REA. You're alive.
AEMILIAN. These scars . . .
REA. . . . are my scars. I love them. Every wound is mine, too. (*She takes his hand and holds the forearm to her lips.*) I kiss the torn flesh. I make it whole. (*He wrenches his arm from her, sudden anguish.*)
AEMILIAN. Don't! We can't. It's done. Our day is over. Rea, get a knife!
REA. A knife? What for?
AEMILIAN. A woman can fight with a knife as well as a man.
REA. No, no. We mustn't fight any more. We've lost. Our soldiers are all gone.
AEMILIAN. Soldiers are people. People can fight. There are still people here in this palace. Women, slaves, children, politicians. Give each a knife.
REA. But that would be foolish. We must surrender to the Goths. We've no choice.
AEMILIAN. I surrendered to the Goths. I had no choice. Well, look at me. Look what they've done to me! Rea, take a knife.
REA. You frighten me.
AEMILIAN. Do you know the word duty?
REA. Yes. Duty to you.
AEMILIAN. Duty to your country?
REA. Yes. Duty to that. Only . . .
AEMILIAN. Which duty is stronger? To Rome or to us?
REA. To us.
AEMILIAN. Rea!
REA. (*Turns away.*) Rome. Duty to Rome.
AEMILIAN. You said the words yourself: "Unhappy daughter of a line of kings." Rea, take a knife. Be ready to do your duty.

REA. That was just a play. That was tragedy.
AEMILIAN. This is tragedy.
REA. No. I won't let it be. (*She tries to embrace him; he thrusts her away; she nearly falls.*)
AEMILIAN. (*Fiercely.*) Take a knife! (*She looks at him at first stunned; then with growing horror.*)
REA. Yes. You *have* come back to me someone else. But I know who you are. (*Wonder, terror.*) Yes . . . yes. I know you now.
AEMILIAN. (*Softly.*) The knife.
REA. . . . I see the empty eyes, the dreadful smile. You are what we fear in the night. The shadow at noon. You are Death! (*Rea turns abruptly and goes into the palace. Aemilian looks after her a moment; his strength recedes a little; wearily, he passes his hand across his eyes, his mouth. Then with an effort he turns Offstage as Tullius crosses to him.*)
TULLIUS. Aemilian, sorry I didn't recognize you, old fellow. Good to have you back. Welcome home.
AEMILIAN. Why aren't you armed? Why aren't you ready for the Goths?
TULLIUS. Now, look. I know you've gone through a lot and we are all terribly, terribly proud of you, but please don't ever think we've been having an easy time of it here at the palace, with all the confusion, and the shortages. Especially paper. Do you realize the Emperor is forced to write his decrees on— (*Holds up paper.*) the backs of unpaid bills?
AEMILIAN. Have you ever seen Ottaker?
TULLIUS. The Gothic butcher? No, fortunately. And I hope I never shall.
AEMILIAN. He is a destroyer. A monster . . .
TULLIUS. True, true, in fact, only the other day I was saying, "Ottaker is a monster." (*Otto Rupf marches in from* R.)
RUPF. Well, sir, your Empire isn't worth a plugged denarius. And the bookkeeping! Worst mess I ever saw!
TULLIUS. A little untidy, perhaps.
AEMILIAN. Who is this man?
RUPF. Otto Rupf. President and Chairman of the Board of Rupf Pants and Vest.
AEMILIAN. What do you want?
RUPF. A straight answer to my proposition. I can still save

the Empire . . . though it's going to be a bit more expensive than I thought.

AEMILIAN. Save the Empire?

RUPF. But I'll keep my end of the bargain. Rupf's word is his bond. Now where's that Emperor? I'm a busy man. Time is money.

AEMILIAN. Is this some sort of lunatic?

TULLIUS. Certainly not! Ottaker will go back to Germany for ten million. This gentleman is willing to give us the ten million.

AEMILIAN. On condition?

TULLIUS. That the Princess Rea becomes Mrs. Otto Rupf.

AEMILIAN. Send for her.

TULLIUS. Send for her? But I'm not at all sure . . .

AEMILIAN. And assemble the court. Assemble the court. That's an order, Tullius. (*Hand on dagger.*) Quick! (*Tullius exits* U. C. *Aemilian turns to Rupf.*) You will have your answer immediately, oh maker of pants.

TULLIUS. (*Off.*) Assemble the court. Court assemble. Assemble. Assemble. Assemble the court . . . ! (*Titus reappears* R., *staggering.*)

TITUS. I'm ready to drop. A hundred, hundred hours, no sleep. Tired. Tired. (*He sits stool* R. *Julia and Rea enter* U. C.)

JULIA. Aemilian. We thought you were dead!

AEMILIAN. (*Kneeling* R. *of* C.) I am dead.

JULIA. Yes, of course. (*She moves down off platform to him.*) We're all so happy to have you back. But nine years is a long time and things are not what they were, and . . . ah, there's dear Mr. Rupf. (*She steps to Rupf. Metellus enters* R. *Zeno from* R. *Tullius from* U. C.)

RUPF. Empress, you're bankrupt.

JULIA. Oh, dear.

RUPF. But I still plan to go ahead with the merger.

JULIA. Oh, good!

RUPF. A deal's a deal.

JULIA. Rea, come and say hello to Mr. Rupf. (*Rea steps down* L. *to him.*)

RUPF. Nice to meet you, young lady. Real pleasure. Real pleasure. (*He takes her hand and kisses it. Aemilian steps* D.)

JULIA. You are such a gentleman. Isn't he, Rea? Isn't he good? And kind? (*She steps to Aemilian, urgently.*) Aemilian,

you must understand our position. You must be reasonable. I know it's a shock to you— (*Voice rises.*) —Rea falling in love with Mr. Rupf . . .
REA. Mother!
AEMILIAN. (*On bench* R., *to Rea.*) Come here.
JULIA. (*As Rea moves to him.*) Careful!
AEMILIAN. (*To Rea.*) Do you love me?
REA. Do I love death? If death is Aemilian, I love death. (*Rupf steps down at* L.)
RUPF. What's this?
JULIA. (*Sternly.*) Rea! (*Pleadingly.*) Aemilian, *help* us!
AEMILIAN. Love with all your soul?
REA. With all my soul, I love you, Death.
AEMILIAN. Would you do anything I asked you to do?
REA. Name it. I will do it.
AEMILIAN. (*Swinging up to* R. *of bench.*) Then marry this fat fool and bear him children as fat and foolish as he!
TULLIUS. Oh, God!
JULIA. (*To Rupf.*) He didn't really mean that, of course, about your weight and intelligence. It's just a way they learn to talk in the army.
RUPF. Oh, I know the sort. Just envy, that's all. Quite used to it. When you close a big deal like this, you learn to take the rough with the smooth.
AEMILIAN. Now give the clown your hand. (*Julia swings Rea to Rupf.*) Otto Rupf, the daughter of all the Caesars will be your wife.
RUPF. (*He steps to Rea, seats her on bench* R. *Aemilian moves to* U. C. L.) Princess, you have to believe me when I say how moved I am. Really moved. These tears are real tears of happiness. Rupf Incorporated . . . (*Shakes hands with Metellus, Tullius and Zeno.*) . . . now stands organically at the pinnacle of the business world. Rupf Incorporated has done it again. The competition will be fit to be tied!
METELLUS. The Empire is saved without a battle.
TULLIUS. We must save the archives. (*He steps* R. *and calls.*) Stop the burning!
ZENO. All together now in a hearty voice: three hozannahs, and one jubilation!

CROWD. Hozannah! Hozannah! Hozannah! Jubilation! (*Achilles calls from* R.)
ACHILLES. Make way for the Divine Caesar! (*Romulus, Achilles and Pyramus appear.*)
CROWD. Hail, Caesar! Hail! Hail! (*All drop to their knees except Julia and Aemilian.*)
ROMULUS. Hail. I must say, everyone seems to be in a good mood. Why?
AEMILIAN. Hail, Caesar, Emperor of three meals a day. Lord of the Chickens. All hail, to the one we soldiers call "Romulus the Little!" (*There is a gasp of horror.*)
ROMULUS. When people become rude to one's face, it is obviously a sign that one's day is just about over.
PYRAMUS. Shall we execute him, Divine Caesar? (*Romulus examines Aemilian carefully.*)
ROMULUS. Aemilian. I might have known.
AEMILIAN. You are the only one to have recognized me. Not even your daughter knew me.
ROMULUS. (*Quickly.*) But never doubt her love. It's just that the vision of age is sometimes more acute than that of youth. You're thin. You've been hungry.
AEMILIAN. While I starved, you ate well.
ROMULUS. Quite true. Welcome, Aemilian.
AEMILIAN. I'm sorry, Divine Caesar. My manners are rude. I've been a prisoner too long. I've forgotten court etiquette.
ROMULUS. You cannot offend me. I see by your hand that you were tortured.
AEMILIAN. I was tortured while you raised chickens.
ROMULUS. Yet which of us, do you think, was the more usefully employed?
AEMILIAN. When I escaped in the North, I walked from one end of Italy to the other. I saw it all.
ROMULUS. Tell me about my empire, Aemilian. I've never seen it, you know. I never leave Tivoli.
AEMILIAN. I saw the ruin of a world.
ROMULUS. And my subjects?
AEMILIAN. Our people are looted and raped by Gothic soldiers; they are cheated by profiteers. And there is no justice.
ROMULUS. (*Thoughtfully.*) No justice. . . . Yes, I have heard these same reports.

AEMILIAN. But how can you know what you have never seen?

ROMULUS. I have . . . imagination. Now come inside. My daughter has waited long enough.

AEMILIAN. I am unworthy to be received by her.

ROMULUS. You are not unworthy.

AEMILIAN. But I am. Humiliated! Treated like an animal by the Goths! Forced to crawl naked beneath a bloody yoke!

REA. Aemilian . . . (*Rea embraces Aemilian. He pushes her back.*)

AEMILIAN. Rea, go to our savior. (*Rea crosses to Rupf.*)

ROMULUS. Savior? What are you talking about? Rea, come here this minute. (*To Rupf.*) I shall attend to you presently, Mr. Rupf.

AEMILIAN. Not presently. *Now.* Rupf will save us all. Through our shame, Rome will survive. Give him your blessing, Caesar. He is not only your savior. He is about to become your son-in-law.

JULIA. Heaven be praised! Dear Mr. Rupf, I welcome you into the family.

RUPF. (*Moved.*) May I call you . . . Mother?

JULIA. Of course.

RUPF. Me, Otto Rupf, son-in-law to the Emperor. A dream come true!

JULIA. (*To Rea.*) Child, you have saved Rome! Believe me, your sacrifice will be remembered. . . .

RUPF. (*Taken aback.*) Sacrifice? Now really, Mother, I'm not exactly what you'd call the worst husband in the world. By a long shot. After all, I'm rich. Good-looking, in an organic sort of way, everyone says so. . . .

ROMULUS. Shut up, fool! We do not sanction this marriage. It will not take place. (*Consternation.*)

RUPF. (*Stricken.*) But . . . Dad!

REA. (*To Romulus.*) Father, I have to marry him. I *must* marry him. It's what Aemilian wants.

JULIA. You cannot stop her.

ROMULUS. Indeed I can. And will. I am still Emperor, for a little while longer. I am also your father. You will do as I tell you. Now go inside this minute.

REA. You see, Aemilian? He will not let us have your comic ending. (*Rea starts to go off* U.)
JULIA. (*Venomously, to Romulus.*) You . . . idiot!
AEMILIAN. You realize that this is the end of all of us? (*Rea pauses at Romulus' side.*)
ROMULUS. No. The beginning. Of your life with Rea. You love her. She loves you. . . .
AEMILIAN. (*Erupting.*) Love! *Now?* Listen, little Emperor. I also bring you news: Rome, the city of Rome, has fallen. (*Alarm. Much muttering. The sky darkens. Far-off cries begin to sound, mournful and strange.*)
ROMULUS. (*Softly.*) At last.
AEMILIAN. The Goths have taken the city. They will be here tomorrow. Ottaker will be here tomorrow. The butcher will be here in your palace tomorrow! He will have your head! He has said he will have your head, on a pike, tomorrow! (*Horror from the assemblage. Repetition: "The monster, the butcher! the killer!"*) Only Rea can save us. There is still time. (*A hush. A long expectant moment.*)
ROMULUS. There is no time left for Rome. But there is time for you. There is time for Rea. There is time for life. Take it.
AEMILIAN. I cannot.
ROMULUS. (*Thoughtfully.*) You are . . . perverse, Aemilian. You have been dishonored, or so you think.
AEMILIAN. I have been dishonored. I know.
ROMULUS. Your body . . . your flesh, abused by enemies.
AEMILIAN. Abused. Tortured. Broken.
ROMULUS. Humiliated?
AEMILIAN. Humiliated.
ROMULUS. And now you want your revenge?
AEMILIAN. Yes!
ROMULUS. But revenge not on the enemy. Not on the Goths. You want your revenge on Rea.
REA. Father!
ROMULUS. Yes, my dear. He wants you hurt, abused, humiliated, as he was. The only way he can love you now is to see you defiled the way he was defiled. He would give you to this creature in order that he might revel at the thought of your shame. Lust at the thought of you in that fat embrace. . . .
AEMILIAN. (*Near breaking.*) Stop!

REA. Aemilian, is it true what he says?

AEMILIAN. I don't matter. You don't matter. But Rome does.

ROMULUS. (*With finality.*) Rome does not matter now. (*He turns to the astonished court.*) It is too late to patch together this falling time. The Emperor knows what he is doing when he throws his empire into the flames, when he lets fall what is already broken and buries what is already dead! This marriage will not take place.

JULIA. Romulus!

ROMULUS. That is my will. (*A long sigh from the assemblage. Romulus turns, more lightly, to Pyramus and Achilles.*) And now I think we've had enough chatter for one day. So, back to work! Pyramus, the chicken feed! (*Pyramus hands him the basket. Romulus starts scattering grain as he exits* R., *accompanied by Pyramus and Achilles.*) Here, Augustus, Tiberius, Claudius. . . . Here, Trojan, Hadrian, Pertinax. . . . Here, chicky chick chick. . . . (*The sound of firing off stage.*)

CURTAIN

ACT TWO

Scene 2

Night of the same day.
There is a moon. In the center of the audience chamber a bed has been set, with mosquito netting.
Romulus, in a dressing gown, appears in the garden from R.

ROMULUS. (*Thoughtfully.*) The last night. The last look at the last moon. Then tomorrow and the last sun. Then . . . what? (*Pauses, touches a leaf, a flower.*) Green . . . red . . . Will there be color? Or just blackness. The thing is done. The pattern is almost complete. (*Holds out hand.*) Am I afraid? The hand is steady. (*Touches flower.*) Even so . . . what is next? (*During this speech Aemilian, in black cloak, enters from* L., *dagger in hand. The entrance of Pyramus and Achilles from* U. C., *carrying torches, causes him to hide behind a col-*

umn. Looks up.) What's that bed doing here? (*Aemilian slips off stage.*)
ACHILLES. It is the best we could find, Divine Caesar.
PYRAMUS. The Empress . . .
ACHILLES. May she live a thousand years. . . .
PYRAMUS. Has sent your bedroom furniture on to Sicily . . .
ACHILLES. General delivery . . .
ROMULUS. Why did she send *my* bed?
ACHILLES. Apparently it belonged to her father.
ROMULUS. How sentimental of her. Well, it's a warm night. This is quite pleasant.
PYRAMUS. The Empress has just requested audience.
ROMULUS. Audience not granted. No visitors tonight. Except my daughter. (*Romulus notices he still wears wreath; he gives it to Pyramus.*) Oh, my poor old laurel wreath. I must have had it on in the bath. Hang it on that peg, will you? (*Pyramus does so.*) How many leaves are left?
PYRAMUS. Only two, Divine Caesar.
ROMULUS. Not only has it been a sad day . . . it has been an expensive one. (*Sighs, then a deep breath.*) Fresh air at last! The smoke's all gone. I must say, disastrous though the day was, at least we got the archives burnt. Probably the greatest contribution I could have made to history.
PYRAMUS. Historians will forever lament Divine Caesar's decision.
ROMULUS. Nonsense. If there is anything an historian hates, it is a fact. I have now set their imaginations free. Henceforth, the story of Rome will be a department of creative writing! (*He sits on divan.*) Bring me my Catullus. I shall read a few lines. (*Pyramus and Achilles look away.*) Or has my wife packed the library because the library belonged to her father?
PYRAMUS. She has done exactly that, Divine Caesar.
ROMULUS. Then pour me some wine. At least the wine did not belong to her father . . . unfortunately. We've drunk all those splendid years. (*Pyramus pours wine. Julia comes in* U. C., *pushing Achilles out of the way.*)
JULIA. Out of my way! Romulus, you will see me!
ROMULUS. Not only will I see you, I *do* see you.
JULIA. You cannot keep me out. Pyramus, Achilles, withdraw.
ROMULUS. Stay.

JULIA. (*Fiercely.*) I am *hereditary* Empress: Achilles . . . Pyramus, obey! (*They go.*)

ROMULUS. Don't you think you're pressing your luck a bit, Julia? After all, I am still capable of an act of domestic violence. In the great tradition of my predecessors.

JULIA. Kill me! I couldn't care less, only let Mr. Rupf marry Rea and save Rome.

ROMULUS. No. Such a marriage would be unthinkable. Did you hear him today? He called me "Dad." It was chilling.

JULIA. Then you must come with us to Sicily. Tonight.

ROMULUS. The Emperor does not flee. Did Tullius find you a proper boat?

JULIA. No. A raft.

ROMULUS. A raft? Oh, dear. You'd better not go. You know you're a bad sailor. You'll be horribly seasick. Also, rafts are dangerous.

JULIA. Far more dangerous to stay here. With you. I shall re-assemble the government in Sicily. We shall fight on against the enemy, at all costs. We must, for the sake of all mankind!

ROMULUS. What a sense of theatre you have! Come off it, Julia. You're going to fight for yourself.

JULIA. Myself? I have no self. I am Rome.

ROMULUS. Are you really? I was never quite certain.

JULIA. If you don't come with us, the Goths will kill you.

ROMULUS. It would certainly be out of character if they did not.

JULIA. I see. (*A new tack.*) Romulus, we have been married twenty years. We were in love.

ROMULUS. What an extraordinary thing to mention! I thought your particular field was politics. Certainly not marital relations. Julia, you shock me! I've never heard you make such a . . . *personal* remark to anyone.

JULIA. If I have been impersonal, it is because you wanted it so. Nevertheless, we were in love once.

ROMULUS. You are stark-staring mad.

JULIA. Do you mean to say that you married me *only* to become Emperor?

ROMULUS. No, that is not what I meant to say. But now *you've* brought the subject up: yes, that *is* why I married you.

JULIA. You dare to tell me this to my face?

ROMULUS. I would certainly never say it behind your back. In my way, I try to be a gentleman. But I believe I do not exaggerate when I say that our marriage has been as close to hell on earth as any marriage I have ever heard of.

JULIA. And for that hell on earth, I hate you.

ROMULUS. And I like you for that. Hate is a pure emotion. But do give me credit for never once having pretended to love you. We were both very practical people. I married you to become Emperor. You married me to become Empress. There is something very clean about that. The motive in each case was intelligent self-interest.

JULIA. True. We needed each other then, and we need each other now. Romulus, you must come with me to Sicily. We belong together, whether we like it or not. It is our destiny.

ROMULUS. I think not. I made you Empress and that's quite enough destiny for you. Your schemes paid off.

JULIA. And what about your schemes? Have they paid off?

ROMULUS. They are about to. Today you said that you had never understood me. I was struck by that. And now that we are both in this curious mood of candor, let me say that I have never understood you. I have never understood people who were ambitious for personal power.

JULIA. (*Scornfully.*) Never understood it? *You?* My dear Romulus, you married me to make yourself master of Rome. If that was not personal ambition, what was it?

ROMULUS. Necessity. What was an end for you was a means for me. I became Emperor for a certain purpose through political cunning.

JULIA. Political cunning! During the whole of your reign you have done nothing but eat and sleep and raise your damned chickens. Not once have you appeared in the city of Rome. You have sat here in this house absolutely still, as the state collapsed about us. Your only gift is your wit which manages to crush opposition. Political cunning! Nero and Caligula in their madness were statesmen of vision compared to you! You do nothing! You are nothing!

ROMULUS. But don't you see, Julia? *That* is my political cunning: that was my plan: to do nothing. Nothing at all.

JULIA. You didn't have to become Emperor to do nothing.

ROMULUS. Of course I did. Otherwise my idleness had no meaning. To be idle as a private citizen would have been perfectly useless, and rather immoral.

JULIA. While to be idle as an Emperor merely endangers the state?

ROMULUS. Exactly. (*Julia is startled.*)

JULIA. What do you mean by that?

ROMULUS. (*Aroused, excited.*) I mean that you have at last, after twenty years, discovered the secret of my idleness.

JULIA. (*Slowly.*) You *deliberately* wanted to endanger the state?

ROMULUS. Yes, Julia. Deliberately.

JULIA. But why? The state is necessary.

ROMULUS. I don't deny the necessity of the state in general. I just deny the necessity of *this* state. Our state. Rome.

JULIA. If you thought that, then why did you, of all people, want to become Emperor?

ROMULUS. Because only an Emperor can liquidate an Empire.

JULIA. And that is why you married me?

ROMULUS. That is why I married you.

JULIA. From the beginning, you wanted Rome destroyed?

ROMULUS. From the beginning.

JULIA. You have consciously and knowingly sabotaged all efforts to save us.

ROMULUS. Consciously and knowingly.

JULIA. You have played the cynic, the clown, the buffoon simply to trick us.

ROMULUS. I should not have put it quite that way, but you seem to have got the general point. (*A pause.*) At last we understand each other, Julia, the masks are down.

JULIA. You are mad!

ROMULUS. No, I am just. (*More lightly.*) Anyway, the work of my life is nearly complete and I wouldn't alter it . . . for the world!

JULIA. Mad! (*She turns to go.*)

ROMULUS. (*Rises.*) Good-bye, Julia. Have a nice trip. Sicily should be great fun this time of year. Especially the beach. But don't get too much sun all at once. You know how easily you burn. (*Julia pauses at* U. *door.*)

JULIA. What you have done you will regret. You cannot play Fate. You are not God. As you have judged us, so shall you be judged. And I pray that when you are, you will be shown no mercy. (*Julia goes. Romulus sits for a moment thoughtfully. Then he picks up his goblet; it is empty. He claps his hands. Pyramus enters.*)
ROMULUS. Pyramus, more wine.
PYRAMUS. Yes, Divine Caesar. (*Pyramus pours wine. His hand shakes.*)
ROMULUS. My dear fellow, you're shaking like a leaf. What's wrong?
PYRAMUS. Divine Caesar does not like us to mention the military situation to him.
ROMULUS. No. I don't like it at all. I discuss military affairs only with my barber. He is the one person I know who seems to understand such things.
PYRAMUS. Divine Caesar, the palace guard has deserted.
ROMULUS. Very well, grant them the title: "The Heroes of Tivoli."
PYRAMUS. They fled because the Goths are just a few miles from Tivoli.
ROMULUS. That is no reason for spilling good wine, and staining my dressing gown.
PYRAMUS. A thousand apologies, Divine Caesar.
ROMULUS. I'm sorry. Go to bed. (*Pyramus goes. Achilles enters. He stands at the* L. *door.*)
ACHILLES. The Princess Rea begs audience of Caesar.
ROMULUS. Oh, my dear, I am glad.
REA. (*Entering* L.) Mother wants me to go to Sicily tonight. With her. But I don't want to leave you.
ROMULUS. Darling, we must all do things we don't want to do. You must go where you'll be safe.
REA. Father, Aemilian says we can still save the state.
ROMULUS. How curious that tonight everyone should want to talk politics. Lunch is the time for politics. Not after supper.
REA. What else should I talk about?
ROMULUS. There are special things a girl talks to her father about at night. Such as: what is closest to her heart.
REA. Rome is closest to my heart.
ROMULUS. You no longer love Aemilian?

REA. Oh, yes.
ROMULUS. But not as much as you did.
REA. More! I love him more than life.
ROMULUS. Then talk to me about Aemilian.
REA. Aemilian says I must marry Otto Rupf.
ROMULUS. My dear, Otto Rupf has a certain appeal. I don't doubt it. I particularly like his money. But you don't love him and even if you did, he makes me uneasy.
REA. He will save Rome.
ROMULUS. But that's exactly what makes me uneasy. Any pants manufacturer who wants to save the Roman Empire must be a bit mad. Or an incurable romantic. Of course, businessmen tend to be romantic. Sentimental. Impractical. Business is often the last refuge of the artist. Nevertheless . . .
REA. Father, there's no one else *can* save us!
ROMULUS. True. But a country which can be saved only by money is a lost country anyway. After all, what *is* the choice, really? On the one hand: catastrophic capitalism, and on the other, a capital catastrophe. (*Sits up.*) Where's Pyramus? I must get him to write that down.
REA. But no matter what, my country comes first.
ROMULUS. Dear girl, you've been reading too much tragedy.
REA. I couldn't live without my patriotism.
ROMULUS. Could you live without your young man? Yes. Perhaps. It is harder to keep faith with a human being than with a country. My darling, forget your play-acting, marry Aemilian and make yourself . . . and your father . . . happy.
REA. Aemilian has rejected me.
ROMULUS. I don't believe it.
REA. He knows what I must do. That's why he doesn't love me any more. He loves Rome.
ROMULUS. Well, luckily for you, Rome is about to perish. Then he will have nothing left to love but you. You'll get him back. I promise.
REA. I'm so afraid.
ROMULUS. Then you must learn to conquer your fear. That is the one art we can master in this twilight time. To look at things as they are, without fear. To do the right thing, no matter how hard, without fear. I've spent my life practicing *not* to be afraid. You practice, too. You know, Rea, you are

all that I have ever allowed myself to care for. (*Rea throws herself into his arms, in tears.*) And I care for you in spite of myself because I've known all along what was to come. I knew how it would end and I wanted to regret nothing.

REA. How will it end? (*Romulus pushes her away.*)

ROMULUS. As it ought. Now. No more tears. Remember what I've told you. And look at me for the last time.

REA. No . . . no! Come with us! To Sicily. Father . . . please!

ROMULUS. No, my dear. If I were to survive, my life would be a complete failure. It would lack . . . *symmetry*.

REA. (*Smiles in spite of herself.*) And you think *I* play-act.

ROMULUS. (*Smiling.*) You have a point there. Yes, I play-act, too. We're very much alike, aren't we? But my performance is necessary. Now go, be brave. . . .

REA. Please . . .

ROMULUS. (*Silences her.*) Forget Rome. Marry Aemilian. Be a woman. Be happy. Quickly now, no more speeches. No tears. Go! (*Rea goes. Romulus looks after her thoughtfully. He picks up a goblet of wine which catches the reflection of Aemilian slipping into the chamber from* U. C. *Aemilian hides. Romulus claps his hands. Pyramus enters from* L.)

PYRAMUS. Is the Divine Caesar ready to retire?

ROMULUS. No, not yet. Pour another goblet.

PYRAMUS. Another . . . ?

ROMULUS. Yes. There's someone else I must talk to. (*Pyramus fills a goblet on the table.*) Now, off to bed with you. (*Pyramus bows and withdraws. Without turning.*) All right, Aemilian. We're alone at last. (*Aemilian emerges from the shadows.*)

AEMILIAN. How did you know I was here?

ROMULUS. I saw you reflected in the goblet. Pyramus keeps them beautifully polished, don't you think? Have some wine. It's poured. Sit down.

AEMILIAN. I stand.

ROMULUS. As you please. Isn't this rather late for a visit? It's midnight.

AEMILIAN. Some visits are made only at midnight.

ROMULUS. How ominous you make it sound! Nevertheless, I

am ready for you. With a delicious wine. Let us drink to each other's . . . health.
AEMILIAN. So be it.
ROMULUS. And to your return from slavery.
AEMILIAN. And to what I must do this night.
ROMULUS. To that. By all means to *that!* (*They drink.*)
AEMILIAN. And now a toast to justice, Divine Caesar!
ROMULUS. Oh? I hope you realize that justice on earth is relative. And sometimes terrible.
AEMILIAN. As terrible as my scars?
ROMULUS. To justice. (*They drink.*) I suppose you will leave with Rea tonight?
AEMILIAN. (*Carefully.*) I hope we shall not be forced to leave.
ROMULUS. You know she loves you. Take good care of her when I'm gone.
AEMILIAN. When you are gone, she will be taken good care of. (*Aemilian comes closer to Romulus. Romulus steps back towards his bed. There is a scream. Tullius appears from under the bed, wringing his hand.*)
ROMULUS. Good heavens, what was that?
TULLIUS. (*Reproachfully.*) You stepped on my fingers . . . Caesar.
ROMULUS. Tullius! I *am* sorry. But how was I to know you were *under* my bed?
TULLIUS. (*Gabbling.*) Well, I just happened to get under the bed to work on my new tax program, completely voluntary, of course. I have the memorandum right here. (*Tullius gets to his feet during this. He is also in a black cloak.*)
ROMULUS. Look! Your hand is bleeding.
TULLIUS. Oh dear! I must have scratched myself on the dagger . . . I mean the *pen* I was writing with.
ROMULUS. (*Politely.*) Such a sharp pen, for such a sharp and astute political mind.
AEMILIAN. (*Ominously.*) Does the Divine Caesar wish to call the palace guard?
ROMULUS. How can I? They've fled. As you well know. But we must get something to bandage poor Tullius' hand. (*He crosses to cupboard L. Opens it to reveal Zeno hunched over.*)

Zeno! I didn't know you liked to sleep in closets. I'm sorry I waked you. Go back to sleep.
ZENO. (*Emerges.*) No, no. That's all right. I'm wide awake now. I'm afraid it's got to be a habit with me, closets. I've had to put up with so many hardships since I left home that I feel, well, more *comfy* in a closet.
ROMULUS. I couldn't be sorrier, disturbing you like this.
ZENO. (*To Romulus.*) Don't let me interrupt.
ROMULUS. Perfectly all right. We're just . . . burning the midnight oil. (*Gives Tullius the cloth.*) Here, Tullius. Bandage your hand. I can't bear the sight of blood. (*Tullius takes cloth.*) Now if there is anyone else hidden in my bedroom, will he—or they—please come forth. (*Metellus appears, wearing a black cloak.*)
METELLUS. Just happened to be in the neighborhood and thought I might drop in and chew the fat with you about this total mobilization thing. (*From the opposite side of the stage, the Chef appears in black cloak, white hat. Romulus is for the only time grieved.*)
ROMULUS. *Et tu*, Chef? (*The Chef joins the semi-circle which now surrounds the Emperor, who is* D.) All of you wear black, I see. I suppose that is the proper shade for conspiracy.
AEMILIAN. Black is the color of midnight and of justice.
ROMULUS. I'm sorry to have put you all to such great inconvenience. Poor things, you've spent half the night under beds and in closets, in the most complicated positions! And as for those extraordinary costumes—why even you, Tullius, look sinister. I'm proud of you.
TULLIUS. We want to talk to you.
ROMULUS. I suspected you had something like that in mind. (*Romulus sits.*) The Emperor is ready to hear his loyal subjects.
TULLIUS. We demand the return of the provinces.
METELLUS. The return of the legions.
CHEF. The return of good living.
AEMILIAN. The return of the Empire.
ZENO. The return of classical culture.
ROMULUS. The Emperor is accountable to no man.
AEMILIAN. But *this* Emperor owes Rome an accounting.
ZENO. Yes, Romulus, you must vindicate yourself before his-

tory. You must explain why you have allowed barbarism to engulf us.

METELLUS. You must explain why you have allowed our military power to collapse.

AEMILIAN. You must explain . . .

ROMULUS. (*Cuts through him.*) There is nothing to explain. If I had conquered the world with your help, you might be entitled to talk as you do. But I have lost a world which you did not win.

TULLIUS. But you let go what was left.

AEMILIAN. You had no faith in us.

ZENO. You refused to believe we are great.

ROMULUS. We were great. But that was before any of *us* were born. To be wise is to be able to recognize a fact. The fact is that Rome is lost. And now that that world is finally lost, I am free and you are no concern of mine, any of you. You are just . . . moths, dancing around the light I give, shadows which will vanish when I no longer shine.

AEMILIAN. (*Suddenly.*) The light! (*The conspirators extinguish the torches, only the candle beside Romulus illuminates the room.*)

ROMULUS. For only one of you have I compassion. Aemilian. (*Aemilian approaches.*)

AEMILIAN. Remember, Romulus, *you* are on trial.

ROMULUS. No. Not I. You. Your midnight court has been convened, but *I* sit in judgment. I will speak to you, Aemilian, as one man to another, as father to son.

AEMILIAN. It is too late in the night to win me, Romulus.

ROMULUS. Win? There is nothing to win. You are quite lost. Yet I do care for *you*, Aemilian, even as I pass sentence. I understand you. I pity you. For you are that perennial phenomenon, the human being who is sacrificed to the state. Your body twisted, your mind twisted . . . out of pity I will answer only to you.

AEMILIAN. Then answer.

ROMULUS. Ask the question.

AEMILIAN. What have you done to prevent Rome from being humiliated as I was humiliated?

ROMULUS. Nothing. (*The conspirators move closer to Romulus.*)

AEMILIAN. Then I accuse you of having betrayed Rome.
ROMULUS. No. Rome betrayed herself. Long ago. Rome knew truth, but chose power. Rome knew humaneness, but chose tyranny. Rome debased herself, as well as those she governed: that is a double curse. You stand, Aemilian, before the throne of the Roman Emperors. That throne is not visible to you, is it? To any of you. But it is most visible to its occupant, to me, its *last* occupant. This throne is set upon a mountain of empty grinning skulls, streams of blood gush upon the steps to this high place where Caesar sits, where I sit, presiding over these cataracts of blood which are the source of power. And now you want an answer from this high place where I sit upon the bodies of my sons and the hecatombs of my enemies. Very well, you shall have your answer. Rome is old and weak and staggering, but her debt is not yet paid nor her crimes forgotten. But the hour of judgment is near. The old tree is dying. The axe is ready. The Goths have come. We who have bled others now must ourselves be bled. You have asked for justice. (*Rises.*) I shall give it! I sentence Rome to death!
AEMILIAN. Hail, Rome! (*All draw their daggers. They close in on Romulus.*)
CROWD. Kill him! Kill him! Kill him! Kill him!
AEMILIAN. Here is justice, Caesar. The knife!
VOICES. (*Offstage.*) The Goths are coming! Run! Help! Fire! Save us! (*The conspirators panic. In a moment all have escaped from the room, scattering in different directions. Pyramus and Achilles enter distraught.*)
ACHILLES. Is the Divine Caesar hurt? (*Romulus, breathing hard, shakes his head.*)
PYRAMUS. (*Looking after conspirators.*) Traitors! Traitors!
ROMULUS. No, not traitors. It is too late, even for treason. There are only victims now. . . . Where are the Goths exactly?
PYRAMUS. (*Jittery.*) In Tivoli, in the town, Divine Caesar. (*Romulus crosses to table, pours wine.*)
ROMULUS. Then why all the screaming? They won't get to the palace until morning. (*A sleeping man rolls out from under the bed; Romulus groans.*) Oh, no, not another one! Who is it? (*Achilles peers at the sleeping figure.*)
ACHILLES. It's the young Prefect, Titus.
ROMULUS. (*Smiling.*) Asleep at last.

PYRAMUS. Shall we remove him?
ROMULUS. (*Turns away.*) No. Let him be. Put a blanket over him. He has no luck, poor man. (*Pyramus puts a blanket over Titus. Then Pyramus and Achilles start to leave.*) Oh, Pyramus . . .
PYRAMUS. Yes, Divine Caesar?
ROMULUS. When Ottaker the Butcher arrives, show him in directly. With style. (*Romulus drinks. The servants bow, withdraw. The light falls.*)

CURTAIN

ACT THREE

It is the morning of March 16, 476. The scene is the same as in the first act. All the busts are gone, saving "Romulus."

Achilles and Pyramus are tidying up. They have a number of wilted laurel wreaths they drape here and there in the room.

ACHILLES. A lovely morning!
PYRAMUS. It is amazing how the sun dares to rise on a day of such despair.
ACHILLES. Nature was always unreliable.
PYRAMUS. Only think for sixty years, under eleven Emperors . . .
ACHILLES. We have served Rome.
PYRAMUS. I simply cannot believe that the whole thing should end in our lifetime. What a lot of dust!
ACHILLES. Fortunately, no one can accuse us of not doing our part. When we go, they will say: That is the end of antiquity.
PYRAMUS. And the beginning of . . . what is the word, Achilles?
ACHILLES. "Modern." The beginning of the modern.
PYRAMUS. I predict this . . . "modern" era will be known as the dark ages.
ACHILLES. No doubt of it. (*Suddenly.*) I hear him. Will you tell him, or shall I?
PYRAMUS. You! I cannot give him such tragic news. (*Romulus enters u. c. in robe and laurel wreath.*)
PYRAMUS and ACHILLES. Hail, Caesar!
ROMULUS. Hail! I'm late. There was an enormous crowd at the audience this morning. Everyone wants a visa or a pass-

port. I can't think where they expect to go. (*Looks about.*) My, you've tidied up nicely. Quite festive! I hope our friend the Gothic Butcher appreciates our efforts. Where's my breakfast? I'm hungry.

PYRAMUS. In a moment, Divine Caesar.

ROMULUS. I hope I don't look too haggard. . . . (*Romulus gets gloves, watering can* U.)

ACHILLES. The Divine Caesar never looked more glorious!

ROMULUS. I don't think I slept more than an hour last night. That young prefect not only snores, he grinds his teeth. What did you do with him? (*He waters* D. R. *tub.*)

PYRAMUS. We placed him in the garden.

ACHILLES. He is still asleep.

PYRAMUS. Does the Divine Caesar know that the Goths have surrounded the palace?

ROMULUS. Yes. (*Crosses to tub* D. L.) Do you know I believe I did more ruling last night than I have in all the twenty years of my reign. (*Notices table.*) What ugly plates! All chipped and cracked. Where is the Imperial service?

ACHILLES. The Empress took it with her last night.

ROMULUS. Ah, yes. It was her father's. Well, perhaps broken plates are more fitting for a last meal. There was a storm early this morning, wasn't there?

PYRAMUS. (*Nods.*) At about dawn.

ROMULUS. Poor Julia. She never was a good sailor. She must have suffered. (*Suddenly.*) Why is it so quiet? I have the odd feeling we're alone. Absolutely alone here. Just the three of us. (*Pyramus and Achilles are* D., *on benches, frightened.*)

PYRAMUS. We are alone, Divine Caesar.

ACHILLES. We are all that's left.

ROMULUS. But where is Tullius? Where's Metellus? Where's my chef?

PYRAMUS. They left with the Empress for Sicily.

ROMULUS. Oh? The government-in-exile, of course. And my daughter, Rea?

ACHILLES. She is gone, too.

ROMULUS. With the Empress?

PYRAMUS. With the Empress.

ROMULUS. And Aemilian? (*He puts down can, removes gloves.*)

PYRAMUS. He is with the Princess.

ROMULUS. Good. Good. At least one thing has worked out well for us. They will marry. They will be happy. (*He crosses to table.*)

PYRAMUS. No, Divine Caesar. They will not marry. They will not be happy.

ACHILLES. They were all drowned. (*Romulus turns slowly* D.)

PYRAMUS. This morning.

ACHILLES. In the storm.

PYRAMUS. The raft was dashed to pieces.

ACHILLES. Near Ostia.

PYRAMUS. The Empress, the court, all are dead.

ACHILLES. A fisherman brought us the news while you were holding audience.

ROMULUS. (*Slowly.*) My daughter Rea and Aemilian dead. (*He looks at them.*) I see no tears in your eyes.

ACHILLES. We are old.

ROMULUS. True. You will die very soon yourselves, in the normal course.

PYRAMUS. Yes, Divine Caesar.

ROMULUS. And I shall die, too. Even sooner. Today, in fact. The Goths will kill me. So he who is about to die would be somewhat . . . excessive to mourn the dead. Serve the morning meal, Pyramus. (*Pyramus removes cover from plates. Romulus breaks into egg; he makes an effort to regain his old wryness.*) Naturally, Augustus laid nothing.

ACHILLES. Nothing, Divine Caesar.

ROMULUS. Tiberius?

PYRAMUS. None of the Julians laid anything.

ROMULUS. Then whose is this?

PYRAMUS. Marcus Aurelius, as usual.

ROMULUS. Did no one else lay?

PYRAMUS. (*Nervously.*) Only . . . Ottaker.

ROMULUS. Really?

PYRAMUS. *Four* eggs today, Divine Caesar!

ROMULUS. (*Delighted.*) Good Heavens! That chicken has achieved greatness. Bestow upon her the title. . . . No, never mind. We have given our last title. (*Swallows wine.*) I must say you both look frightfully solemn.

ACHILLES. Divine Caesar, Otto Rupf has offered us positions in his household at Rome.

PYRAMUS. At the vulgar sum of four thousand a year. With three afternoons off a week.

ACHILLES. With such leisure, we would have time to write our memoirs.

PYRAMUS. "Backstairs with the Twelve Caesars."

ACHILLES. The serial rights in Britain alone would keep us comfortably in our sunset years.

ROMULUS. I must say, if destiny did not have other plans for me, I might apply for a job with Mr. Rupf, too. . . . You are free, of course. (*They cough, with embarrassment.*) Oh, I forgot. (*He takes off laurel wreath, breaks off last two leaves, and gives one to each.*) The last two leaves from my crown. The last financial deal of my reign. They are yours. I must say I have never been more at peace than I am now, when everything is over.

PYRAMUS. Does the Divine Caesar wish the Imperial Sword of Alexander?

ROMULUS. Didn't we pawn it?

PYRAMUS. No pawnbroker would take it. Too rusty. We had already picked out the jewels. Shall I fetch it?

ROMULUS. No, dear Pyramus. It would be out of character. I prefer to go to my fate as I have lived, with a knife and fork, not a sword. (*War cries are heard in the garden.*) What on earth is that?

ACHILLES. The Goths, Divine Caesar. They are here!

ROMULUS. Well, I'm afraid I shall just have to receive them at breakfast. (*Pyramus and Achilles are both terrified.*)

PYRAMUS. Is everything satisfactory, Divine Caesar?

ROMULUS. Yes. You have done your work well. Now you both may go. (*They start to go* R.) Oh, when you write your memoirs, don't forget to mention that the last Emperor at his last meal ate heartily.

PYRAMUS and ACHILLES. Hail, Caesar! (*They withdraw, bowing.*)

ROMULUS. Hail. (*He continues to eat thoughtfully, occasionally sipping wine; as he does, a Goth enters, a lean, middle-aged man dressed in trousers, a light trench coat and a broad-brimmed hat. He is quite relaxed, but curious. He wan-*

ders about the room, as though visiting a museum. The only martial note is a sword, strapped rather haphazardly over his coat. Romulus watches him curiously, still eating. The Goth does not notice him. He stands looking up at the bust of Romulus. But then a large muscular youth in battle gear enters, accompanied by three soldiers who take positions guarding the room. The young man sees Romulus, draws his bayonet and crosses—grinning fiercely—to Romulus, who remains very still.)

YOUNG MAN. Die—Roman! (*He is about to bring the sword down on Romulus' head when the Goth turns to him.*)

GOTH. Stop that!

YOUNG MAN. Yes, dear Uncle.

GOTH. (*Indicates scabbard.*) Bayonet!

YOUNG MAN. Yes, dear Uncle. (*Young man and soldiers sheathe their bayonets.*)

GOTH. (*To Romulus.*) Well?

ROMULUS. Well . . . ? Oh, welcome to Tivoli. (*Doubtfully.*) You are Goths, aren't you?

GOTH. Can't you tell?

ROMULUS. As a matter of fact, no. According to Tacitus, all Goths have fierce blue eyes, long blond hair, and enormous muscles. Frankly, I'm disappointed. You look like a Byzantine botanist.

GOTH. We're both disappointed. Romans always run away from us. You are the first not to be frightened.

ROMULUS. I dare say there are misconceptions on both sides. Are you by any chance wearing trousers?

GOTH. What else?

ROMULUS. Such a remarkable garment! Where do you button it?

GOTH. In the front.

ROMULUS. How practical. (*He drinks.*)

GOTH. What are you drinking?

ROMULUS. Asparagus wine.

GOTH. Oh? (*Goth takes goblet.*)

ROMULUS. It's home-made. (*Goth drinks, shudders.*)

GOTH. Good God! We must show you Romans how to make beer. I congratulate you on your Venus. That one down by the pond as you turn into the driveway.

ROMULUS. What about it?

GOTH. What about it? An original signed by Praxiteles. Worth a fortune.

ROMULUS. I have all the luck! I thought it was just a copy and now the art dealer's gone back to Utica. This is the last blow.

GOTH. I was told you had a fine collection of busts. Where are they?

ROMULUS. I sold them yesterday.

GOTH. Too bad. I wanted them for my palace. (*Romulus looks at him with wonder.*)

ROMULUS. Then you . . . *you* are Ottaker?

OTTAKER. (*Nods.*) Prince of the Goths.

ROMULUS. Well . . . well. We meet at last. How do you do? I am Romulus. You know? Emperor of Rome? SPQR?

OTTAKER. I knew who you were.

ROMULUS. I can't think how. That portrait they use on my coins was done years ago. Now I suppose you will need my head to decorate that pike of yours. I am ready. (*He rises.*)

OTTAKER. Good. Very good. You are brave. But first let me present my nephew. Bow, Theodoric.

THEODORIC. (*Bows.*) Yes, dear Uncle.

OTTAKER. Deeper, nephew.

THEODORIC. Yes, dear Uncle.

OTTAKER. In fact, get down on your knees before the Emperor of Rome.

THEODORIC. Just as you say, dear Uncle. (*He is on his knees.*)

ROMULUS. Don't you think you're rather overdoing it?

OTTAKER. Now leave us. (*The soldiers leave.*) You, too, nephew.

THEODORIC. Yes, dear Uncle.

OTTAKER. Wait outside.

THEODORIC. Just as you say, dear Uncle. (*Theodoric goes.*)

ROMULUS. He will never forgive you for that.

OTTAKER. What do you think of him?

ROMULUS. What do *I* think of him? Well, a very polite young man. Yes, I was favorably impressed.

OTTAKER. Were you really? I'm not surprised. He is very polite. "Yes, dear uncle. Just as you say, dear uncle." He is a teetotaler. He sleeps on the floor. He never goes out with girls. He practices every day with bayonet. At this very moment, he is outside there in the hall doing push-ups. He is perfect.

ROMULUS. In every way a classic hero.

OTTAKER. You recognize the type. Naturally. You are classic, too. (*He holds up his sword.*)

ROMULUS. I am glad we're going to do this privately.

OTTAKER. My people worship Theodoric. He is their ideal. He dreams of just one thing, the conquest of the world. You understand that, don't you?

ROMULUS. Yes. We used to have heroes like that. In fact, that's how we got started. Now would you prefer to kill me here, or in the garden?

OTTAKER. Completely immaterial. . . . Theodoric has inspired us all.

ROMULUS. I'm sure he has. I would prefer it here, but if you have other plans, don't let me . . .

OTTAKER. (*Irritably.*) Don't rush me. You've heard of Gothic-ism?

ROMULUS. Oh, yes. We hate it, of course. But I've often wondered what it was.

OTTAKER. Theodoric invented Gothic-ism.

ROMULUS. But what is it?

OTTAKER. Make a guess.

ROMULUS. A rationale for the Gothic conquest of the world.

OTTAKER. Correct.

ROMULUS. Which is to say: nothing?

OTTAKER. Go to the head of the class.

ROMULUS. I was always good at examinations. Look, if we're going to chat, do you mind if I finish breakfast? It's getting a bit cold.

OTTAKER. Go right ahead. (*He sheathes sword.*)

ROMULUS. Thank you. (*Sits; continues to eat.*) We used to have Roman-ism. But since we're so much older than you, we dropped the word. We now refer to "the sacred heritage of classical culture." We conquered the world in order to give everyone a classical education. At least that's our story now. I'm not sure the world was grateful. But then, you should know. You were one of the races we educated.

OTTAKER. Oh, yes. You were great educators. You taught us everything: greed, political murder, injustice.
ROMULUS. I am sorry. For what it is worth, I *am* sorry. Rome and I ask forgiveness for the past. In fact, I offer myself as final payment.
OTTAKER. Good. Reasonable. Acceptable. Yes. You are just. (*A start.*) What was that?
ROMULUS. You seem rather jumpy. I'm quite alone here. You're perfectly safe. (*Ottaker prowls, looking into cupboards.*)
OTTAKER. I thought I heard him.
ROMULUS. Heard who?
OTTAKER. Theodoric.
ROMULUS. He makes you nervous, doesn't he?
OTTAKER. Nervous? You presume too much! Theodoric is a hero. Because of him I have conquered the world. Because of him my people have become a nation of heroes.
ROMULUS. A terrible fate—if I may say so—not only for the world, but for the heroes.
OTTAKER. (*Stops.*) Yes. You are wise. Why do I doubt it? After all, I admired your book, "The Moral Principle in History."
ROMULUS. Really? The original version or the abridged?
OTTAKER. The original. I read all of it.
ROMULUS. How remarkable! No one here has ever got past the first chapter.
OTTAKER. But authors are seldom as good as their books. Now, one last question . . .
ROMULUS. You do make it sound like an examination.
OTTAKER. That is exactly what it is. You are being examined, and graded.
ROMULUS. Graded? Like an egg?
OTTAKER. Like a man. (*Suddenly.*) Do you know about eggs?
ROMULUS. Poultry is my passion. (*Ottaker takes egg from plate, examines it.*) Yes. Do have an egg.
OTTAKER. From an Anatolian hen?
ROMULUS. That's right. Are you a chicken-breeder?
OTTAKER. (*Absorbed by egg.*) Yes.
ROMULUS. What a coincidence! So am I!
OTTAKER. You?

ROMULUS. For twenty years.
OTTAKER. Those your chickens out there in the yard?
ROMULUS. Yes. Some are Anatolian. Some from a new breed in Gaul.
OTTAKER. Do they lay?
ROMULUS. Do you doubt it?
OTTAKER. Judging by this egg, no, not well. . . .
ROMULUS. You're right. And just between us chicken-breeders, I'm a bit worried. They lay less and less. Only one hen is really up to the mark.
OTTAKER. The gray one with the yellow spots?
ROMULUS. How did you know?
OTTAKER. She's the best. I brought that particular breed into Italy. Wanted to see how it would do in a warm climate.
ROMULUS. Then congratulations! It's done marvelously well.
OTTAKER. Thank you. My *own* breed.
ROMULUS. Oh. Then you must be a poultry man of the first rank.
OTTAKER. As Sovereign Father of my people, I occasionally tend to useful matters. (*Serious again.*) Now the last question: What do you think of *me?*
ROMULUS. (*Carefully.*) I thought of you as the Gothic Butcher. The Scourge of God. Now I see you are just a chicken breeder like myself.
OTTAKER. The examination is complete. (*Both rise. Ottaker draws his sword.*)
ROMULUS. You will find me ready. You may proceed. I have had my breakfast. Would you prefer that I stood, or was seated?
OTTAKER. Immaterial.
ROMULUS. I shall sit. (*He sits beside table; closes eyes.*)
OTTAKER. My spies told me that Romulus was brave.
ROMULUS. Cowardly . . .
OTTAKER. Wise . . .
ROMULUS. Foolish . . .
OTTAKER. Just . . .
ROMULUS. I have *tried* to be just.
OTTAKER. I didn't believe them.
ROMULUS. Your information agencies are as inaccurate as ours. Now, Ottaker, let us close the book of Rome.

OTTAKER. Very well. (*He raises his sword; then he drops to his knees.*) Divine Caesar, I have come here with my army to subjugate myself and all the Goths to you. Take my sword. I surrender! (*Romulus looks at him with amazement.*)

ROMULUS. Surrender? You're out of your mind! Here! Stop that. Get up this minute. I don't want your sword.

OTTAKER. Because I am Gothic does not mean that I cannot be led by intelligence.

ROMULUS. But this is all wrong. This *can't* happen. For Heaven's sake, get up off that floor.

OTTAKER. (*Rising.*) We have discussed chickens intelligently. Agreed?

ROMULUS. Agreed.

OTTAKER. Then why can't we discuss our two countries intelligently?

ROMULUS. Because it is not done.

OTTAKER. May I sit, Divine Caesar?

ROMULUS. I don't find that at all amusing. Of course you may sit. You are the conqueror. I am the conquered.

OTTAKER. That was a moment ago. Since then I surrendered to you. (*He sits at table.*)

ROMULUS. If only my poor wife could see me now! I who baffled everyone for twenty years am now completely mystified by a Goth. Go right ahead. Sit down. Have some asparagus wine. No, that's right, you don't like it. I'm afraid we have no beer. Have an egg.

OTTAKER. I am perfectly serious.

ROMULUS. So am I when I say you must kill me.

OTTAKER. Why?

ROMULUS. Because that is my fate. Because that is the way I have planned it.

OTTAKER. Your are not God.

ROMULUS. No. But . . . Curious. My wife said the same thing.

OTTAKER. Why are you so eager to die?

ROMULUS. Ottaker, when I was young I looked about me and saw an old world crumbling, this world. On every side I saw forms without use, prayers without faith, laws without justice. And I said to myself: This must come to an end. But not in the usual gradual deadly way, but all at once . . . *I* would bring it down. And in its fall men might see a lesson. See justice for once on earth give perfect measure.

OTTAKER. There is no such thing.

ROMULUS. Just before you arrived, I was told that my daughter was dead, because of me. But I did not weep. Because I knew that I would die, too. I myself would expiate Rome's sins. Now you propose to rob me of my fate? No. Not even the Gothic Butcher could be that cruel.

OTTAKER. Your grief will pass.

ROMULUS. You are afraid. (*He forces sword upon Ottaker.*) Now then, conquer your fear. Do it!

OTTAKER. I cannot kill you. (*He ignores the sword.*)

ROMULUS. I must say your reputation as a butcher is quite undeserved.

OTTAKER. Have you any idea what will happen to me if you refuse to become our leader?

ROMULUS. Yes. You will be known as the man who conquered the world. Ottaker the Great. You will be much admired.

OTTAKER. No. I shall be murdered.

ROMULUS. Well, that is an occupational hazard. To be taken in stride.

OTTAKER. The oracles all agree that one day Theodoric will say: *No*, dear Uncle. And that will be the end of me.

ROMULUS. I never interfere in family matters.

OTTAKER. And when I'm gone, Theodoric will build a new Rome. More monstrous, more terrible than the old. And you will have sacrificed yourself for nothing.

ROMULUS. I am interested in the past, not the future. In moral example, not in political demonstration.

OTTAKER. Romulus, save me.

ROMULUS. Certainly not.

OTTAKER. Then save the human race from Theodoric.

ROMULUS. My work is done. (*He tries to press the sword into Ottaker's hands.*) Now, in the name of Heaven, will you complete this farce?

OTTAKER. Certainly not. (*Romulus lets the sword fall with a crash.*)

ROMULUS. All right. I shall fetch Titus. He is in the garden. He will do it. (*He starts toward the garden.*)

OTTAKER. (*Roars.*) Stop! (*Romulus stops, smiles.*)

ROMULUS. You *are* master here. . . . You see?

OTTAKER. All right. You force me to rule. I shall force you to live.

ROMULUS. But if I live, my life has been a failure.

OTTAKER. Let me be the judge of that. If the world was as you thought it was, your remarkable experiment might have had some meaning. But the world is not neat. The world is not a book. Life is a river, a flood. You cannot change its course. You were not there at its beginning. You will not be there at its end. So live, Caesar.

ROMULUS. Live . . . *live* . . . now? The work of twenty years come to nothing? No.

OTTAKER. You insist upon being classic, don't you? (*Takes sword.*) Then I shall be classic, too. I shall begin my new reign with a murder. (*Starts to go* U.)

ROMULUS. What murder?

OTTAKER. I shall do to Theodoric what he plans to do to me.

ROMULUS. Stop! That would be foolish.

OTTAKER. Foolish? Necessary.

ROMULUS. No. Better the enemy you know than a thousand you do not. You can keep an eye on one, but not on many.

OTTAKER. Then you are interested in what becomes of me? That means you are interested in life. Good. Good.

ROMULUS. You weren't going to kill him. That was a trick.

OTTAKER. (*Shrugs.*) He does mean to have my head.

ROMULUS. But he may not get it. The future is most unreliable as I have discovered. There is no way of controlling it.

OTTAKER. (*Carefully.*) Do you mean to say that I cannot judge the future?

ROMULUS. No one can judge the future.

OTTAKER. Then can anyone judge the past?

ROMULUS. No. No one can judge the past. (*He is immediately aware of his own logic; he is horrified.*) Oh, God! I sacrificed what was left of Rome because I hated its past. You were willing to sacrifice your Goths . . .

OTTAKER. Because I fear their future.

ROMULUS. Yet if you were really afraid, why did you conquer the world? Why did you murder thousands of men and women in the name of . . . nothing?

OTTAKER. Public opinion. Theodoric wanted war. He convinced my people they wanted war. They forced me to mobilize. But I thought if *I* took charge of the army, we could at least have a humane war.

ROMULUS. You were naïve.

OTTAKER. I know that now. My army has been brutal. Cruel. No worse than any other army, but even so I've been shocked by what we've done. I tried to quit. I was willing to accept that fellow's offer . . . what's his name . . . makes pants?

ROMULUS. Otto Rupf. Who will, I promise you, inherit this earth.

OTTAKER. Yes. I thought I could bribe my officers while they were still corruptible. But the closer we came to the city of Rome, the more they believed in Gothic-ism.

ROMULUS. Which is nothing.

OTTAKER. Which is nothing.

ROMULUS. You have no power over the future. I had no power over the past.

OTTAKER. And now we are both helpless. Time has us by the throat.

ROMULUS. There is only one thing left.

OTTAKER. There is nothing left.

ROMULUS. Ah, but there is. The present. The day. The moment. The instant. *Now*.

OTTAKER. Go on. . . .

ROMULUS. Given the present . . . and the two of us . . . here . . . in this room, there is a great deal we can do.

OTTAKER Name it!

ROMULUS. First, a treaty of peace.

OTTAKER. What are the terms?

ROMULUS. Well, I might make you Emperor of Rome. . . .

OTTAKER. No. No. You are the last *Emperor*.

ROMULUS. Oh, yes. That's right. We mustn't rob me of my one small distinction. I've worked very hard to be the last. Then I shall make you *King* of Italy. How's that?

OTTAKER. But how long will I reign? How long before Theodoric . . .

ROMULUS. The present . . . remember? The past is a dream. The future does not exist. Since we cannot have perfection, we must make do with imperfection.

OTTAKER. We are human.

ROMULUS. We are human.

OTTAKER. And there are no absolutes?

ROMULUS. No absolutes. Only the long present . . . the now. So let us begin, Ottaker, to live now.

OTTAKER. Without great expectations.

ROMULUS. But without despair.

OTTAKER. The conditions of the peace treaty?

ROMULUS. The simplest. You and I—two mistaken men who came to their senses—we will make it safe to breed chickens from one end of Europe to the other. Historians will snub us, of course. Not enough battles. But ours is the true glory.

OTTAKER. Brief glory.

ROMULUS. But make the moment good and who knows *what* will come?

OTTAKER. I am a pessimist. But I will be led by you.

ROMULUS. And now let us as sovereigns act as if all the accounts in the world were finally balanced, as though spirit had finally triumphed over matter.

OTTAKER. (*Shouts.*) Theodoric! (*Theodoric appears with pike.*)

THEODORIC. Yes, dear Uncle?

OTTAKER. Summon the chiefs of staff.

THEODORIC. *But*, dear Uncle . . .

OTTAKER. (*To Romulus.*) What did he say?

ROMULUS. I believe he said, "But, dear Uncle."

OTTAKER. That's what I thought he said. Yes, Theodoric?

THEODORIC. Here is the pike.

OTTAKER. So?

THEODORIC. (*Points to Romulus.*) And there is his head.

OTTAKER. Naturally.

THEODORIC. But his head should be *on* the pike.

ROMULUS. (*To Theodoric.*) I'm sorry. I did my best to put it there for you.

THEODORIC. Dear Uncle, we *must* have his head. We owe it to our people. We owe it to Gothic-ism.

OTTAKER. Nephew: What are the four great virtues of Gothic-ism?

THEODORIC. Perfect courage. Absolute sincerity. Complete faith. Total obedience.

OTTAKER. Then, nephew be perfectly courageous. Accept

things the way they are. Be absolutely sincere. Do not plot against me. Have complete faith. That all things are for the best. Be totally obedient . . . (*Roaring.*) . . . and summon the chiefs of staff!

THEODORIC. (*Terrified.*) Yes, dear Uncle. (*He runs off* R.)

ROMULUS. Very impressive, Ottaker. You handled that marvelously well. But aren't you afraid that one day he might . . .

OTTAKER. The present. Remember?

ROMULUS. You are a good student. What an odd feeling to be alive. I'd quite got used to death.

OTTAKER. It's a pleasant feeling, life.

ROMULUS. Yes. I'd almost forgotten. We must *never* forget that, Ottaker. In fact, I shall write it down this very minute. "Life is good." If I can find a piece of paper. (*Rupf enters with Pyramus and Achilles, who are wearing pants, followed by Theodoric and Gothic soldiers. They are in field uniforms, worn and dusty.*) Ah, Mr. Rupf. How reassuring to see you on the job.

RUPF. The early bird gets the worm.

ROMULUS. Organically speaking.

OTTAKER. (*Resonantly.*) Goths! Dusty, tired, burned by the sun, your duty is done at last. Gothic-ism has triumphed! (*Three cheers: "All hail! All hail! All hail!"*) Before you sits Romulus, the Emperor of Rome. Salute him. (*The men salute.*) There he is. The man you mocked. The man you sang your songs about. The enemy of Gothic-ism. Yet I have come to know his quality. His greatness. You will never see his like again. You will never see a greater man, no matter *who* my successor is. (*Theodoric scowls.*) Speak to us, Divine Caesar. (*Romulus rises.*)

ROMULUS. Thank you for that generous introduction. And now watch while the Emperor of Rome dissolves his Empire. (*With his hands he designates an imaginary sweeping globe.*) For the last time look upon this great world, floating in air, set spinning by the breath from my lips. Look upon those green and fertile lands set in the blue sea, with its dolphins and sudden storms—rich provinces yellow with grain, tall cities swarming with life. Look upon this Rome, (*Contracts the imaginary globe.*) this sun which at its zenith consumed the earth with fire . . . now a toy in my hand, which I let drop, and vanish into nothing. (*There is a moment of almost devotional silence.*

The Goths are mystified.) Ottaker, Prince of the Goths, I name you King of Italy. (*All kneel.*)
OTTAKER. For my part, I grant Romulus the villa of Lucullus. As well as a pension of six thousand gold pieces a year.
ROMULUS. (*Smiles.*) The lean years have ended. (*All rise. Romulus removes laurel wreath and places it on Ottaker.*) The laurel wreath. What's left of it. It goes with your new position. You are now King. Such is the will of the Senate and the people of Rome. SPQR. You will find the Senate, if you want them, in the Catacombs. They will come out if you grant them unlimited debate. I always did. Talking keeps them out of mischief. You will find the people of Rome going about their usual business. Tell them you're in charge now. They won't mind. Goodbye, Ottaker. Be a good King. And remember about life. . . .
OTTAKER. I will remember.
ROMULUS. The present is all that we have. Make it good.
OTTAKER. (*To everyone.*) Hail, Romulus the Great!
GOTHS. Hail, Romulus, the Great! (*Suddenly Titus rushes on stage from* L., *sword drawn.*)
TITUS. Down with the Emperor! Where is he? Let me kill him! Where is the Emperor? (*Ottaker steps between Titus and Romulus.*)
OTTAKER. Put down that sword. There is no Emperor.
TITUS. No Emperor? But there he is.
OTTAKER. That is a chicken breeder from Campania. The Empire was dissolved some minutes ago.
TITUS. (*Stunned.*) Rome . . . *gone?*
ROMULUS. (*Gently.*) I'm afraid so. All gone. It was only a dream. Anyway, you finally got your rest.
TITUS. (*Slowly.*) And so the last Roman soldier slept through the end of his world. (*Titus, shattered, sits in a chair, face in his hands.*)
ROMULUS. And on that wistful note, gentlemen, the Roman Empire is at an end. (*Romulus walks off stage as Ottaker and the Goths salute.*)

CURTAIN

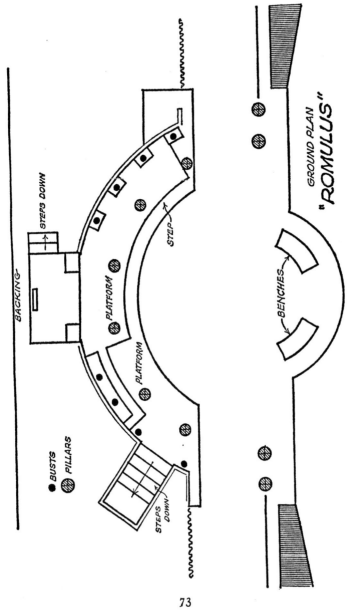

PROPERTY LIST FOR "ROMULUS"

ACT ONE

SET TO OPEN

Furniture
  Tea cart
  Writing desk
  Four small chairs
  One large chair (throne)
  Round table
  Two stools
  Two benches
  Two flower urns
  Two chicken crates
  One chariot flower urn
  Two large chicken feed bags
  Ragged drape

On desk (U. C.)

Visitor's book
Pen

In closet (U. L.)

Money box
Bandage
In flower urn (D. R.)
Two practical blooms

On tea cart (L.)

Four plates
Three egg cups
Three sets utensils
Two goblets
One goblet with napkin
Coffee pitcher
Wine pitcher

Hour glass
Bunsen burner with plate
Tongs
Salt and pepper
Handbell
Fruits in bowl
Tablecloth
Lighter

Smoke gun plugged in (L.)

Caution: fill lighter on cart

Off stage U. C.

Pike
Two fire pots

On bench (U. R. C.)

Watering can
Gardening gloves
Large green cushion
Small chicken feed bag
Two small flower pots
Rea's cape

On throne chair (U. L.)

Toga for Romulus
Wrist bands

Off L.

Large tray with: 3 saucers, 3 cups with coffee, 3 napkins, 1 spoon for sugar, sugar bowl, creamer
Rolls in napkin in silver dish
3 eggs in silver frame basket
One sconce base
Small tray with: candlestick, 2 golden goblets, golden glass decanter
Two wilted laurel wreaths
Portfolio for Tullius
Shield and map for Metellus
Tureen with hand towel
One money bag for Apollonius

Tray with: chipped goblet with wine, 2 chipped saucers, cruet, chipped egg cup, fruits in wicker basket, rolls in wicker basket, wicker basket with 3 small brown eggs, tablecloth, napkin

Off R.

Three cushions
Ladder
Bed and bedding
Taboret with fruit bowl
Foot stool
One sconce base
Two stuffed chickens
One kitchen knife
Briefcase

PERSONAL PROPS

Six bayonets and scabbards (Gothic Soldiers)
Sword and belt (Ottaker)
Roman sword and scabbard (Titus)
Roman sword and scabbard (Tullius)
Roman sword and scabbard (Chef)
Roman sword and scabbard (Zeno)
Roman sword and scabbard (Metellus)
Dagger (Aemilian)
Watch and chain (Pyramus)
Kitchen matches (Pyramus)
Notebook and pencil (Pyramus)
Ring (Aemilian)
Wreath (Romulus)—with removable golden leaves
Magnifying glass (Apollonius)
Sticky labels (Apollonius)
Calling cards (Rupf)
Handbag (Julia)
Scroll (Titus)

Also onstage at opening

Nine busts of the Roman Emperors

ACT TWO
SCENE ONE

Strike

Visitor's desk
Chariot flower cart
Two yellow cushions
Ladder
Tea cart
Sticky labels off busts

Ready Off L.

Smoke gun
Sconce base

Round table with tray, candlestick, golden glass decanter, 2 golden goblets

Set

Rearrange four chairs—one set with its back downstage R. C.
Leave orange cushion U. L. on top step in front of closet
Gloves and watering can under the bench U. R. C.
Portfolio for Tullius on chair L.
Shield leaning against R. C. pillar for Metellus
Map on bench U. R. C. for Metellus

MAKE SURE BANDAGE IS CLEAR ON SHELF IN CLOSET U. L.

BRING LEAF FROM ROMULUS' WREATH TO STAGE MANAGER'S DESK
SCENE TWO

Set

Round table pre-set with tray, candlestick, goblets and decanter moves on from L. to U. L. C.
Orange cushion moves from step U. L. to bed U. R.
Bed, bedding, foot stool, taboret with fruit bowl and handbell moves on U. R.
Rearrange three chairs, one at L. of table, one each stage R. and L.
Sconce bases, one each stage R. and L.
Bedroom drapes

Strike

One chair off R.

Off Stage U. C.

Fire pots lit
Lighter should be with fire pots
 (CAUTION: check lighter for fluid)

CLOSET DOORS SHOULD BE CLOSED

ROMULUS IN PLACE OFF R.

AEMILIAN IN PLACE OFF L.

TULLIUS UNDER BED (WITH MEMORANDUM)

TITUS UNDER BED

ACT THREE

Strike

Bed, bedding, foot stool, taboret with fruit bowl and handbell
Tray with decanter, golden goblets and candlestick
Sconces
All busts except "Romulus" u. c.

Set

Yellow drapes
Laurel decorations strung
Two wilted wreaths on floor d. c.
Watering can, gloves on bench u. r.
Tea cart above stool l. with chipped saucer and egg cup, bunsen, lighter, wicker basket with rolls in white linen, wicker basket with 3 small brown eggs, and the hourglass
Round table is set with chipped goblet half filled with wine, chipped plate, utensils, cruet, wicker basket with fruit, tablecloth and napkin

ROMULUS' WREATH HUNG ON COLUMN STAGE R. IS PLACED OFF STAGE U. C.

CHECK CLOSET DOORS

CHECK LIGHTER FOR FLUID

NEW PLAYS

• **A QUESTION OF MERCY by David Rabe.** The Obie Award-winning playwright probes the sensitive and controversial issue of doctor-assisted suicide in the age of AIDS in this poignant drama. *"There are many devastating ironies in Mr. Rabe's beautifully considered, piercingly clear-eyed work ..." –The NY Times.* "With unsettling candor and disturbing insight, the play arouses pity and understanding of a troubling subject ... Rabe's provocative tale is an affirmation of dignity that rings clear and true." –Variety. [6M, 1W] ISBN: 0-8222-1643-4

• **A DOLL'S HOUSE by Henrik Ibsen, adapted by Frank McGuinness. Winner of the 1997 Tony Award for best revival.** *"New, raw, gut-twisting and gripping. Easily the hottest drama this season." –USA Today.* "Bold, brilliant and alive." *–The Wall Street Journal.* "A thunderclap of an evening that takes your breath away." *–Time.* "The stuff of Broadway legend." *–Associated Press.* [4M, 4W, 2 boys] ISBN: 0-8222-1636-1

• **THE WAITING ROOM by Lisa Loomer.** Three women from different centuries meet in a doctor's waiting room in this dark comedy about the timeless quest for beauty – and its cost. *"... THE WAITING ROOM... is a bold, risky melange of conflicting elements that is ... terrifically moving ... There's no resisting the fierce emotional pull of the play." –The NY Times.* "... one of the high points of this year's Off-Broadway season ... THE WAITING ROOM is well worth a visit." *–Back Stage.* [7M, 4W, flexible casting] ISBN: 0-8222-1594-2

• **MR. PETERS' CONNECTIONS by Arthur Miller.** Mr. Miller describes the protagonist as existing in a dream-like state when the mind is "freed to roam from real memories to conjectures, from trivialities to tragic insights, from terror of death to glorying in one's being alive." With this memory play, the Tony Award and Pulitzer Prize-winner reaffirms his stature as the world's foremost dramatist. *"... a cross between Joycean stream-of-consciousness and Strindberg's dream plays, sweetened with a dose of William Saroyan's philosophical whimsy ... CONNECTIONS is most intriguing ... Miller scholars will surely find many connections of their own to make between this work and the author's earlier plays." –The NY Times.* [5M, 3W] ISBN: 0-8222-1687-6

• **THE STEWARD OF CHRISTENDOM by Sebastian Barry.** A freely imagined portrait of the author's great-grandfather, the last Chief Superintendent of the Dublin Metropolitan Police. *"MAGNIFICENT... the cool, elegiac eye of James Joyce's THE DEAD; the bleak absurdity of Samuel Beckett's lost, primal characters; the cosmic anger of KING LEAR ..." –The NY Times.* "Sebastian Barry's compassionate imaging of an ancestor he never knew is among the most poignant onstage displays of humanity in recent memory." *–Variety.* [5M, 4W] ISBN: 0-8222-1609-4

• **SYMPATHETIC MAGIC by Lanford Wilson. Winner of the 1997 Obie for best play.** The mysteries of the universe, and of human and artistic creation, are explored in this award-winning play. *"Lanford Wilson's idiosyncratic SYMPATHETIC MAGIC is his BEST PLAY YET... the rare play you WANT... chock-full of ideas, incidents, witty or poetic lines, scientific and philosophical argument ... you'll find your intellectual faculties racing." –New York Magazine.* "The script is like a fully notated score, next to which most new plays are cursory lead sheets." *The Village Voice.* [5M, 3W] ISBN: 0-8222-1630-2

DRAMATISTS PLAY SERVICE, INC.
440 Park Avenue South, New York, NY 10016 212-683-8960 Fax 212-213-1539
postmaster@dramatists.com www.dramatists.com

NEW PLAYS

- **SMASH by Jeffrey Hatcher.** Based on the novel, AN UNSOCIAL SOCIALIST by George Bernard Shaw, the story centers on a millionaire Socialist who leaves his bride on their wedding day because he fears his passion for her will get in the way of his plans to overthrow the British government. *"SMASH is witty, cunning, intelligent, and skillful."* –Seattle Weekly. *"SMASH is a wonderfully high-style British comedy of manners that evokes the world of Shaw's high-minded heroes and heroines, but shaped by a post modern sensibility."* –Seattle Herald. [5M, 5W] ISBN: 0-8222-1553-5

- **PRIVATE EYES by Steven Dietz.** A comedy of suspicion in which nothing is ever quite what it seems. *"Steven Dietz's ... Pirandellian smooch to the mercurial nature of theatrical illusion and romantic truth, Dietz's spiraling structure and breathless pacing provide enough of an oxygen rush to revive any moribund audience member ... Dietz's mastery of playmaking ... is cause for kudos."* –The Village Voice. *"The cleverest and most artful piece presented at the 21st annual [Humana] festival was PRIVATE EYES by writer-director Steven Dietz."* –The Chicago Tribune. [3M, 2W] ISBN: 0-8222-1619-1

- **DIMLY PERCEIVED THREATS TO THE SYSTEM by Jon Klein.** Reality and fantasy overlap with hilarious results as this unforgettable family attempts to survive the nineties. *"Here's a play whose point about fractured families goes to the heart, mind – and ears."* –The Washington Post. *"... an end-of-the millennium comedy about a family on the verge of a nervous breakdown ... Trenchant and hilarious ..."* –The Baltimore Sun. [2M, 4W] ISBN: 0-8222-1677-9

- **HONOUR by Joanna Murray-Smith.** In a series of intense confrontations, a wife, husband, lover and daughter negotiate the forces of passion, lust, history, responsibility and honour. *"Tight, crackling dialogue (usually played out in punchy verbal duels) captures characters unable to deal with emotions ... Murray-Smith effectively places her characters in situations that strip away pretense."* –Variety. *"HONOUR might just capture a few honors of its own."* –Time Out Magazine. [1M, 3W] ISBN: 0-8222-1683-3

- **NINE ARMENIANS by Leslie Ayvazian.** A revealing portrait of three generations of an Armenian-American family. *"... Ayvazian's obvious personal exploration ... is evocative, and her picture of an American Life colored nostalgically by an increasingly alien ethnic tradition is persuasively embedded into a script of a certain supple grace ..."* The NY Post. ... *"NINE ARMENIANS is a warm, likable work that benefits from Ayvazian's clear-headed insight into the dynamics of a close-knit family ..."* –Variety. [5M, 5W] ISBN: 0-8222-1602-7

- **PSYCHOPATHIA SEXUALIS by John Patrick Shanley.** Fetishes and psychiatry abound in this scathing comedy about a man and his father's argyle socks. *"John Patrick Shanley's new play, PSYCHOPATHIA SEXUALIS, is ... perfectly poised between daffy comedy and believable human neurosis which Shanley combines so well ..."* –The LA Times. *"John Patrick Shanley's PSYCHOPATHIA SEXUALIS is a salty boulevard comedy with a bittersweet theme ..."* –New York Magazine. *"A tour de force of witty, barbed dialogue."* –Variety. [3M, 2W] ISBN: 0-8222-1615-9

DRAMATISTS PLAY SERVICE, INC.
440 Park Avenue South, New York, NY 10016 212-683-8960 Fax 212-213-1539
postmaster@dramatists.com www.dramatists.com